Make to
Katherine Whitmer

THE GLORY IN A STORY

A joyful journey through memories

Katherine Whitmer

Also by Kathleen Whitmer

GREEN RUBBER BOOTS:
A joyful journey to wellness

FOR THE ASKING:
A joyful journey to peace

ON THE COVER
Geraniums
oil on canvas, 24″ x 46″
by Kathleen Whitmer

TYPE DESIGN
The Glory in a Story: A Joyful Journey through Memories was typeset in
Adobe Caslon Pro, designed by Carol Twombly. It is a revival of the original
designs of William Caslon, first designed and cut in England in the 18th century.

BOOK DESIGN AND PRODUCTION
by Peter Miller
Western Reserve Typographics, Akron, Ohio

PRINTING
by Bill Wyatt
Wyatt Printing, Akron, Ohio

THE GLORY IN A STORY
A joyful journey through memories

Written and illustrated by
KATHLEEN WHITMER

Foreword by
EUGENE LINEHAN, s.j.
Georgetown Prep, Bethesda, Maryland

PEACH PUBLICATIONS, INC.
AKRON, OHIO

THE GLORY IN A STORY:
A Joyful Journey through Memories

FIRST EDITION, LIMITED EDITION

ISBN 0–9661079–5–0

Library of Congress Cataloging-in-Production Data:
    Whitmer, Kathleen.
    The glory in a story: a joyful journey through memories/
Kathleen Whitmer. — 1st ed.
    p. Cm.

    1. Stories. 2. Childhood. 3. Spiritual Biography.
    4. Whitmer, Kathleen. 5. Happiness, 6. Self-Actualization

Library of Congress Control Number: 2005925706

CONTENTS

"Start today making a wonderful
meaningful memory."

AUTHOR

Again I must dedicate this, the third in a trilogy

to my husband

JERRY, *who continues to have faith in me*

and my good friends

PAULINE PERSONS

JOAN STOKES

ALBERTA SCHUMACHER

JEAN TREMELIN

DONAMARI GUY

GRETCHEN GUY

and

FATHER EUGENE LINGHAN, S.J.

and

PETER MILLER

ADAM MILLER

and

BILL WYATT

"Time moves forward except for
memories."

Brian Green

FOREWORD

BY EUGENE LINHAN, S.J.
GEORGETOWN PREP, BETHESDA, MARYLAND

F AITH IS the substance of things hoped for, the evidence of things not seen," so speaks the author of the Epistle to the Hebrews. And it rings through one's memories: how God writes straight, sometimes with crooked lines.

That's my memory of the author. For 26 years I walked as Chaplain through the long corridors of the Clinical Center, the National Institutes of Health. Visiting the cancer institute I came to know and profoundly admire

Kathleen Whitmer. Above all it was her honesty coupled with profound trust in a loving Creator and in the skills of her surgeon. Humor helped and she is blessed with it.

Our author's life mirrors the faith as described in our opening quotation. Such proves for us how God works artistry if only we can say "Amen"; and especially when it hurts. That is the story you will find throughout the pages of Kathleen's book. She can help us see good news in our lives. Visit the wisdom and humor of a life lived fully because each moment is important. Sit back and enjoy a real expert in the job of learning how to be fully human. It is enriching, believe me.

PREFACE

BALANCE IS a word we associate with scales, a teeter-totter, walking, gymnastics, or diet. Yet, that seven-letter word can be used in so many areas of our lives.

What is a balanced day? What is a balanced lifestyle? When is a friendship in balance? When are we balanced in prayer? When is our spending in balance?

It occurred to me not long ago that this, my third book would have as its theme, balance in our lives. While *Green Rubber Boots* centered on wellness and *For The Asking* carried the theme of peace throughout, the third in the trilogy needed to be a reckoning of the importance of balance in our lives. While I do not completely like the harsh sound of the word balance, I am not quite able to come up with quite a better way to describe what I hear people saying and see people living. For a while, I thought perhaps the word should be tranquillity, a nicer, more gentle-sounding word, but tranquillity is close in meaning to peaceful and fails to say what balance says so well even in its own rather awkward-sounding way. I found memories bring about that kind of balance we learned from our early years.

What is a balanced diet? Why is balance so very important in the life of a gymnast? Why does the teeter-totter work best when it is in balance? Have you ever witnessed someone with vertigo trying to walk down a narrow hall?

Without balance, the gymnast falls from the beam; the person on the light end of the teeter-totter hangs on in the air, the person with vertigo veers from side to side in the long hallway, and the unbalanced scales can not weigh correctly.

Life without balance is just the same. Look around at our out-of-balance world. Extremes exist everywhere.

Balance is about our moods, our attitudes, our heroes, our closets, the poor versus the rich, the overweight versus the thin, the prayerful and those who do not pray.

Someplace along the way we allow ourselves to get out of balance: with friends, with food, with exercise and with routines.

Being in balance means we break old habits, plan a new way, buy something in a new color, get out of an ugly rut, look back to a time when our lives were more in balance. We need to work to change, to grow. We move the furniture, see a sad movie, visit a new place, think of someone else rather than ourselves first. Balance needs to include the new and the old to stay in place.

When I hear someone say they bicycle 60 miles a day, or swim 50 laps in what seems an impossible amount of time, or jog six hours a day, I wonder about the things that don't get done. We all have exactly the same number of hours in each day. How we choose to use them and distribute them is how we choose to balance our lives. In this all-or-nothing world, scaled to perfection, we take away the joy that living in balance brings. Run some, play some, be silent sometimes, yell loudly other times. Go to a ball game but don't forget to go to an opera or a ballet. Watch a professional football game yet remember to also enjoy a tee-ball game. Visit an art museum and stop at a gym. Is your spiritual balance in tune with your physical balance? Is equal time being spent on all the areas of your life?

Beware that we do not work hard at one thing and forget all else around us. Have a schedule, yet, be flexible if an old friend visits unexpectedly. Putting balance in your life will lighten life. Refresh your mental skills and challenge your ability to think about what you are doing, buying or eating. Why do you put your feet on the floor every morning? Make the reason a reality. Happy balancing as you now begin to read this, my book of making memories count.

"Joyful memories bring peaceful thoughts."

AUTHOR

to another brings with it a sense of wonder. Will my readers want to read what I write for them? I wonder if my paintings will come together. How will I know when it's time to stop?

At the school where I am the artist-in-residence, the children often ask me, "How do you know when you're done?" I begin by laughing a little, and then I tell them food gets "done," paintings get finished or completed. They laugh. Yet still, they are puzzled at how I know when to stop.

When you think about it, it is an interesting concept. There must be an ending: one last stroke, one last story, one last chapter, one last word. Going too far, just as with cooking a standing rib roast, it is easy to "overdo." There is a delicate balance between completed work and something that has gone too far.

Now that I write, I realize the need for careful timing in all the creative processes. Often, when I am reading, I find some works, have a nice flow and a strong reason for having been written, yet, they seem labored. If there is drudgery in the doing, the repetition, for instance, can become part of the process that can annoy the observer or reader.

We are living in a society that seems to repeat and repeat. People tell the same stories, television tells the same

WHERE DO BOOKS
COME FROM?

As I begin this, my third book, I realize that I feel much the same as I did when I began my first book, *Green Rubber Boots, A Joyful Journey To Wellness*. Writing is a complex art. It brings with it a variety of feelings and emotions. I feel much like I do as I begin a new painting with paint and a clean, white canvas. I feel anticipation, wonder, excitement, joy and anxiety.

The creative process does not have exact answers or predictable results. Moving from one part of the process news over and over again, and people give directions again and again. Perhaps that repeating of information has led to poor listening skills. It is almost as though people think, "I don't have to listen this time, she'll repeat it at least two more times."

I am often asked how I decided to write a book, how long it took, how I knew where to start, whether I was intimidated? Let me quickly walk you through the process.

Life is full of experiences. People like knowing how others think, react and cope. Early after my cancer experience was behind me and I was no longer able to return to my teaching position at Kent State University because of a damaged heart, due to the experimental drug I took during a clinical trial, I found that people were interested in where I had been. They liked knowing about "their hospital," the National Institutes of Health. Few knew the extent of some of the good things done in medical research with their tax dollars.

I finally had time; time to relax, time to think, time to have the quiet we long for when we are on the treadmill of life. That time became the beginning of a whole new career. Little did I realize that illness gave me the ability to be more creative than the usual work I had done all my adult life.

I began speaking to groups: Rotary, Kiwanis and Junior Leagues. The groups gradually got larger. The talks I began giving led me to a variety of groups of people. One talk led gradually to another, then another. I found myself excited and happy with the planning and the presentation of materials that could help others. My teaching skills helped me as I started this new journey.

At one particular talk to a group of people representing the National Tumor Registry Bank, I was scheduled to precede a well-known doctor. He was the keynote speaker. I was his twenty-minute "warm up." I had no problem with the arrangement until I had completed my twenty-minute time slot. The group was large and in the back of the room the lady who had made all the arrangements motioned me to continue talking. The doctor was running late. I relaxed and decided to tell a few stories about some of the people I had met along my cancer journey at the National Institutes of Health. When I saw the doctor arrive, I closed by thanking them for their patience and good listening skills. One little soul in the fourth or fifth row from the front raised her hand. She asked, "Have you ever thought of writing any of this?"

"No, I haven't," I replied. I am a retired art professor and I can hardly spell my own name."

She offered to do all the typing if only I would record some of it. Her sincerity and her offer encouraged me. The seed had been planted. It takes just a few nice people to spark our imaginations. That was the day that I considered becoming a writer. One little seed had been lovingly planted in my brain. It wouldn't go away. And so, one beautiful spring day during our yearly vacation as I sat under a palm tree with a pencil in hand and a tablet on my lap, words began to spill down onto the clean, lined, yellow paper. They wouldn't stop. Entire days slipped by when I did nothing else. A sense of urgency emerged. Like Grandma Moses was with her paints, I was with words and stories. *Green Rubber Boots* emerged!

Writing time became my favorite time of each day. It did not matter if anyone read my work. The joy was in the process. I realized that I knew things which were stored inside me that might help others. Life became more worthwhile. I stumble now and then, go through dry periods, but I simply love the happiness the written word brings me.

"Just whisper the maybes of life."

AUTHOR

GETTING SUNDAY BACK

WRITING HAS brought with it a delightful new joy to my life. I have discovered quite by accident, new sounds of syllables, new combinations of letters, new attention to similarity to the same letters used together with different endings. The letters prefix "re" is an example of what I am trying to describe. Relax, rest, renew, refresh, rejuvenate, rejoice, repeat, refuse, respond, and redeem.

Looking over this list makes me want to look more closely at the meaning and purpose to the similarity of God trying to get us to understand what He wants for us. He likes the letters "re" used together to get us to understand, in a rather simplistic way, that it is His plan to understand and learn and see the need to have a Sabbath... a time of rest. He is trying in His own way to stop us, to get us to step back and see ourselves. What has happened to that day of "re?" What is the rush? Why are we always on the go, always in an overload syndrome? How, for instance, do we get our Sundays back?

I long for the return to my childhood days of rejuvenation. Like reloading the spiritual part of me, my wholeness leans into itself, twisting away the worn and the tired feelings, making room for the ready rush of the renewable.

Satisfaction comes like quiet waves on the beach returning to the sand to remove the debris brought by the rush of the ocean's energy. Smoothly it returns in order to bring forth more of itself. God provides us the puzzle of life that we may sort, search and see the message of where we are to find joy in His words. Writing has helped me to be closer to that level, balanced person I would like to be.

I BELIEVE IN MIRACLES

MOTHER DIED on a New Year's Eve. The holidays have never been the same without her. That sadness of her death changed how we, as a family, celebrated the Christmas season.

The year following her death, we felt the need to change our holiday plans. Since my sister lived on Long Island, we decided to celebrate the blessed event and the beginning of the New Year by being together in New York at her home on Long Island.

The plan was to spend a few days before the holiday in New York City. We have always loved a few days in the "Big Apple" to window shop, watch the skaters at Rockefeller Center and attend Mass at St. Patrick's Cathedral.

Christmas Eve arrived. We had a nice relaxing dinner in the Edwardian Room at the Plaza Hotel. Our window table looked over Central Park. Horse drawn carriages lined 58th Street carrying people bundled in warm plaid wool blankets. It was a beautiful evening. Snowflakes the size of quarters floated softly to the ground.

Our plan was to finish dinner and casually walk down the few blocks on Fifth Avenue to St. Patrick's Cathedral for midnight mass.

We strolled down Fifth Avenue, hand in hand, very aware of the special place where we were. We could see the lighted Cathedral's stained-glass windows glistening through the snowflakes. During our New York visits, we had never missed a visit to St. Patrick's Cathedral. There it stood, safe, as beautiful as ever. We had given what we thought was plenty of time for the walk to our destination. No problem, the Cathedral was always open, always welcoming, a beacon in the night.

We gradually slowed our pace. We had trouble adjusting to what greeted us. The Cathedral was cordoned off with wide yellow tape like that used at the scene of a crime. All doors were closed except for the front double doors.

New York police surrounded the church. A line formed from the open doors and wound around and down 52nd Street. The line was four and five persons across. A line to go to church? We looked in amazement. What we thought was a perfectly planned evening had gone seriously wrong.

A kind policeman must have seen the surprised look on our faces as we studied the situation. After telling him our plans, he laughed, "These people have had tickets for midnight mass for months, some since the first of the year. They're scarce as hen's teeth."

"Wow, I never in all my days needed a ticket to go to church," I explained.

Jerry stood bewildered. "Well, we'll just have to wait until morning to attend services. We can go before your sister picks us up to go to her house for the day." Jerry reasoned.

I was so disappointed. I had looked forward to the beauty and grace of midnight mass on the eve of the birthday of Christ. Sadly, I turned to walk back to our hotel when, out of nowhere, appeared a woman with a beautiful face, whose head was wrapped in a soft, pink wool scarf with a wide band of beautiful knotted fringe. Dark curly hair poked its way out and around her lovely face.

"Were you really looking forward to going to church this evening?" she asked.

"Oh yes," I replied.

"You look so disappointed," she stated.

"I am," I said.

With that, the lady reached out holding two tickets. "Here, take these," she offered. She handed them to me.

"Oh no, I can't take your tickets. What will you use?" I asked.

"Don't worry about me," she said.

With the tickets in my hand, I turned to Jerry. "Look what that nice lady gave me." I said

"What lady?" he asked.

"The lady in the pink scarf with the rosy cheeks," I replied.

"I didn't see any lady," Jerry said.

I turned to look, she was nowhere. He had not seen the person who gave me the tickets to Midnight Mass. Where had she gone? I looked back and around, she was gone. Her lovely translucent face had been as real as Jerry's and the policeman's. From where had she come? Where had she disappeared? Her image with the soft snowflakes falling on her dark lashes had vanished. I had not even time to say thank you.

With that, the kind policeman took us to the open door, to the front of the line.

An elderly gentleman dressed in a morning suit of gray striped trousers, tails and soft gray gloves escorted us to what were to be our seats.

We were bewildered. We were in about the fifth row of the magnificent Cathedral. Candles burned, light flickered. The Cathedral was dressed in all its glory for the celebration of the birthday of Christ Our King.

We sat stunned. We looked questioningly at one another. The organ roared out its loud voice in announcing the arrival of Cardinal Cook. He walked so close to us that we could have reached out and touched him. His magenta vestment glowed in the candlelight.

In his homily, he talked of love, love for one another and love for God, and the love of God who loved us so much that He sent his only Son to us. He came to live among us to teach us how to live life with Him at our core.

After the homily, Beverly Sills of the New York Opera, sang the Hallelujah Chorus from Handel's Messiah. Her clear glorious voice echoed and rippled throughout the vaulted ceiling. It was chilling. The scene was far more than we had ever anticipated. Christmas was at last what it was meant to be. We witnessed it more fully than we ever had before. From out of a New York crowd on that beautiful snowy night stepped an angel armed with two tickets that we two little people from Ohio could use to celebrate the birth of Christ in such a grand setting. We believe in miracles.

"There are memories that surround us, ours is only to be aware."

AUTHOR

A BRAND NEW CAR

IT WAS 1935. The Depression our parents talked about for the rest of their lives was in full bloom. Money was scarce. The things we purchased we cherished. As children, we sat on the floor. The furniture was covered; drapes were pulled so the sun would not fade the fabrics. The furniture was expected to last forever. Nothing was ever thrown away until it was completely worn out. When the iron needed a new cord or a new part, we took it to the repair shop. Repair shops were plentiful. Saturday was grocery store day. Groceries were carefully selected. Not an extra penny was spent. There were no fun foods, snacks or soda pop of many flavors. Times were tough.

Our house was neat and tidy. There was no clutter. Our neighbors' houses were the same. The neighborhood was friendly and people visited one another, often to share the beauty of new gardens planted with delphiniums, daisies, portulaca, and roses in a variety of colors.

One lovely summer day, our neighbor, Mr. Moore, pulled into his driveway. His drive bordered our yard. Behold, he was driving a new shiny black four-door sedan! It was the first new car the people in the neighborhood had seen in years.

A few neighbors came from their porches to get an up-close view. The crowd grew. Ooh's and aah's surrounded the new black beauty. The new car got everyone's attention. It was an unusual event.

As the story goes, Mary Ann, my then five-year old sister decided she didn't like the color of the car. To her, black just didn't seem right.

Daddy was in the process of painting our kitchen. In those days, kitchens were always yellow. He was between the first and second coats. He left the yellow high-gloss enamel in the garage along with some new four-inch brushes.

Everyone was so excited and involved at the admiration of the new car; no one was keeping an eye on Mary Ann. Since she liked the yellow glossy paint in the kitchen, she decided to change the color on Mr. Moore's new car.

As the group dispersed, Mary Ann prepared her tools. Before anyone knew it, she had painted the entire passenger side of the black beauty a glossy-kitchen-paint-yellow. She was proud of her accomplishment. As she rounded the car to start on the other side, my Mother realized what she had been doing! She and the new car were covered in yellow paint. She held the brush tightly in her little hand; drips of paint made a path where she had been. She stood proudly, a huge smile covered her pretty little face. "Come see," she begged my Mother.

Mother began her usual litany of Irish prayers, "Holy Mother of God, please don't let what I think happened be a reality," she prayed.

It was too late. Even prayer couldn't change what Mary Ann had done. The entire side of the "new beauty" was yellow. Enamel paint applied at random, big strokes and little strokes, covered the entire side of the four-door car. Long drips of paint ran down onto the running board. The windows had paint on them. She was fast. Her work was done in determination. She was proud!

My Mother screamed out in horror. Mr. Moore lurched out his front door; the crowd began to reassemble. Their excitement and words of happiness changed to startled, wide-eyed faces of horror.

"What has she done?" they questioned unbelievingly.

What had been a happy summer day had turned into a major disaster!

Over the years, Mother loved telling the story. I adored every detail. It was most fun when we would be driving to Cleveland to see a baseball game. My Mother would answer my pleas to tell it again. Mary Ann would get a long face while we all broke out in laughter-that kind of laughter that only a story told for the fiftieth time can bring. Even Mary Ann would snicker a little towards the end of the worn story.

"How was I to know Mr. Moore didn't want a yellow car? And why wasn't anyone watching me?" she innocently asked.

She was right. Children do need to be watched... carefully!

"Develop the ability to believe in magic... the magic of the child in the child."

AUTHOR UNKNOWN

HOMECOMING QUEEN

IT WAS my first Homecoming Day in college. Fall leaves crunched under my feet.

The walk to the stadium for the big football game between classic rivals was filled with joyful people. Rosy cheeks, warm clothes, bright yellow frying pan-sized mums pinned to the ladies' coats. There were cheers, hot dogs and popcorn. Excitement filled the air.

What a happy time it was! I don't think I watched much of what I had gone to see because I was so enthralled with all the excitement around me.

Half time of the football game arrived. The announcer with the smooth, deep, voice asked for our attention. The trumpet section of the band heralded the special happening that was about to begin. The Homecoming Queen was about to be introduced. Pauline Moore walked onto the field on the arm of the Student Council President. The President of the University, Dr. White, greeted her in the gold circle in the center of the field. He leaned down and kissed her beautiful rosy cheek. Her smile was wide, her white teeth could be seen from my student section seat high in the bleachers. Her arms held a bouquet of roses. There were dark red roses. There had to be at least one hundred of them! She stood queen-like, proud, pretty and perfect as they crowned her. Her crown of gold and fresh mums made her dark black hair even more beautiful than it was. How could that be? She was such a perfect creature. The huge mum pinned to her lapel had long beautiful gold and navy ribbons suspended from it. The ribbons moved gently as the Fall wind blew across the football field.

Oh, the wondrous beauty of it all! Where were her parents? Did she have sisters, brothers and relatives in the stands waving wildly as she was driven around the rim of the football field sitting high in the back of the newest model of the biggest, brightest convertible on the market for all to see and adore? One lovely, poised, gloved hand waved to her admirers. Heaven, is all it was, just plain heaven.

Three years later I was sent by an organization to which I belonged to represent it in the Homecoming Queen judging session. A group of professors and students were to narrow the large group down to five finalists. From that five, the student body was to vote. I borrowed a plain, black dress from my roommate, put on a fresh bit of lipstick, ran a brush through my hair, made sure my Mamie Eisenhower bangs were in order, and reported to the assigned place. I was given a number on a white card much like the cards we take when we are in line at the meat market. I sat on a metal folding chair waiting for my number to be called, hoping it would be soon in order that I could get back to the dorm, return the black borrowed dress and get on with the reason I had gone to college in the first place. My painting course that quarter was taught by a great artist. I wanted him to be happy with my work during our Friday critique session.

Numbers were called in sets of five. Up we went in a neat row. We stood, the judges looked. One by one we were called to the table to respond to the judges' questions. "Why do you want to be Homecoming Queen," Dr. Hoose asked me. She was my Psychology 160 Professor.

A woman with a PH.D. in 1958, standing in front of me. Wow! I respected her bright mind, her tailored clothing and her sensible plain shoes. Her only flair was her glasses. She was married to an ophthalmologist. She had glasses to brighten every day. As we walked to her class, we would jokingly bet on which glasses she would be wearing on that particular day.

The red frames were my favorite. To this day, I search for red framed glasses.

In response to the question "Why do you want to be Homecoming Queen?" I answered, "because I was sent here by my sponsoring group and I guess they wanted it." I was directed to go sit in a lonesome area and told to "stick around." My paint brushes and half completed canvas waited for me as I sat expecting to get eliminated.

While my lonesome area got larger, many were excused, another round of "show and tell" followed. And finally there were just five of us. The rest of the evening included picture taking and interviews. There would be no painting for me that night!

The next day the names were announced along with pictures. I saw all of them far sharper than I. Betty Oliver would surely be the winner. Her snow-white blond hair was the envy of every co-ed on campus.

Good, I could now get on with my life as a student. Money was scarce. Mother and Daddy had worked hard for those dollars it took to send me to school. I must not waste them. "Waste not, want not," was etched in my head.

Several days later, the student body voted. At 8:00 that evening as I cheerfully painted on a large canvas in the art building, my roommates entered announcing, "Everyone's looking for you! You're the Queen!"

I cleaned my brushes, placed my canvas in the canvas bin, returned to my room, put on the borrowed black dress and spent the night in the Photography Department of the School of Journalism. Hot lights, uncomfortable poses, commands from everywhere, lasted until my dorm curfew finally rescued me. By the time I got to the dorm, everyone else had used all the hot water. After a cold shower, I climbed into bed exhausted. Along with the now half-completed painting, I had two chapters of history that needed attention.

History of Civilization was never my strong suit. To this day, I thank God for giving me Professor Black for that mystery of a course. He took pity on my poor spelling and inexact dates of wars and which army did what to this or that country.

The next days were filled with the Homecoming Day crowning ceremony activities. More valuable time was wasted. From my meager wardrobe, I had to select clothing for that wonderful day. I was the Queen. I was going to stand in the Gold Circle in the middle of the field, be kissed and driven around the football field, wear a bright yellow frying pan-sized mum, wave to the crowd. And, I was to wear the gold crown filled with white mums and carry a bouquet of 100 roses. I was to be like Pauline Moore.

Homecoming Saturday morning arrived. The football game was to start at 1:00 so I put on my blue jeans and started to clean my room. I had plenty of time to do the task that I always did on Saturday mornings. The phone rang, "Where are you?" It was the President of the Student Council. He sounded so frantic. "Everyone is waiting for you. You're the guest of honor at the Homecoming Breakfast for the Alumni. The President doesn't want to start without you."

"No one told me," I replied. "I'm cleaning my room."

"Cleaning your room on Homecoming Queen Day?" he screamed into the phone. "Get here in ten minutes." Slam went the phone.

Quickly and without too much fanfare, I re-borrowed the black dress, grabbed my black school coat, put on my only pair of black heels and proceeded to head for the student center for breakfast with the Alumni and the President. The walk was up and down hills across the huge campus.

People in cars waved. University pennants and flags waved out windows of dorms and school transportation buses. I stumbled along as fast as I could. The President's eggs were probably getting cold. My parents were somewhere in traffic. My boyfriend was in his usual Saturday morning law school class. We had arranged to meet at the game — hopefully before half time when I would be heralded by the university band to the Gold Circle in the center of the field.

The dining room was empty. Breakfast was over. Everyone had eaten. "They all left for the stadium," the waitress told me.

"Oh, okay" I replied.

Alone, tired, cold, hungry, I hiked my way miles to the stadium. The man taking tickets wanted mine. I had none. "No ticket, young lady?"

"Nope." I had no ticket. I was the Queen.

"The Queen?" he asked. "Queen of what? Have you any proof?"

Proof, proof? How does one tired soul prove such a thing? I had no escort, no crown, no roses, and not even a bright yellow frying pan-size mum with satin blue and gold ribbons pinned to my school coat.

Someone rescued me with the school paper tucked under his arm. It had my picture on the front page. "That's you OK." In I went.

Someone spotted me in the crowd and grabbed me and rushed me to the waiting gold 1958 Edsel convertible. Most of you reading this don't even know what an Edsel was. It was a car put out by the Ford Motor Company for only two years. It somehow turned out to be a flop and was discontinued. I sat tall on the back of the car. Someone wrapped a wool plaid blanket over my lap.

"She has no mum, she has no mum." someone repeated. "Everyone in the stadium has a mum," another shouted.

"Here, she can wear mine," a generous soul said. I felt obligated to return it after the big half time show ended..

A dozen roses, not the hundred I thought I saw Pauline Moore carrying, were flung into my arms.

"Wave, wave," the Student Council President commanded as he proudly drove the gold Edsel around the track surrounding the football field.

After three years I was living the life of pretty, poised Pauline Moore.

I walked to the center of the field. President White kissed me and the gold crown rimmed in white mums was placed on my head as the packed stadium cheered.

Later in the day, when I removed the crown, I discovered it was made of Styrofoam sprayed with gold paint. Why had Pauline Moore's crown glowed like 24K gold?

Why is life seldom what it seems? Somehow, it was far more fun watching Pauline Moore and imagining all the wonders of her day as Queen than being it myself.

The day ended with a huge dance in the university gymnasium. The pink dress my Mother had bought me fit perfectly. It was really quite pretty. At intermission the leader of the band, Duke Ellington himself, for the famous Homecoming dance walked to my "throne" and kissed me, after I was crowned for the second time with the same styrofoam sprayed gold crown. He kissed me, just as big as you please. It was a warm, wonderful kiss. The crowd roared and clapped.

The day had ended better than it had begun. And now, 46 years later, I have had my moment in the limelight, my claim to fame — I had been kissed by Duke Ellington. The Duke himself kissed me!

It has been fun all these years to tease my Law School boyfriend turned husband that I had been kissed by one of the world's greatest. Duke Ellington saved me from what had been a pretty miserable day.

*"Love for others is as easy
as you make it."*

AUTHOR

THAT LITTLE VOICE

W^E PRAY to be better people. We beg forgiveness for the wrongs we have done. We yearn to be better people. We find ourselves at the end of each day hoping to be better tomorrow. Sometimes, we are not happy with ourselves. We linger in bookstores scanning the self-help section. We have such good intentions. Our desires are sincere. Yet our knowledge and our behavior do not match.

We hear things like, "Be all that you can be." "Start today to be a new you." "You won't recognize yourself."

Being our best selves is as easy as we make it. It means we have to start by simply listening to that wonderful little voice we all have within us. It is a wonderful gift that was given to us at birth. Sometimes it screams at us and other times it just whispers softly. The real secret is learning to take it seriously.

How many times have you started to do something and that little voice warned you not to do it? Yet, since we think we know everything and we live in a constant state of denial, we react. But, thinking we know everything isn't always good enough.

Being that self we so long to be begins with awakening each day and saying aloud, "Today I am going to be the person I was created to be." Saying it over and over throughout the day will help to convince you that along with the good sense of that little inner voice, you will step one more step toward your goal.

"Once upon a time we only dreamed."

AUTHOR

TARGETING
YOUR MARKET

JUST WHY do people reach out for a book? Help me count the reasons. Some people need to be entertained. Some want to think or learn. Some wish to live in a world of make believe. Some search for information, while others search for wisdom. Then there are those who are just plain bored with life. Others only read a book because it was given as an assignment.

I have heard people say they only read on vacation. History buffs read only about the past, while science fiction scans the future.

Some people stick to mysteries, loving that "whodunit" feeling of anxiety, while others like to sob as they turn one tear-stained page after another.

When I began my writing career, my New York agent and publishers told me I had to "target my market." Weeks went by. I kept rehearsing "target your market," in my subconscious. Should I write for men or women, sick or well, rich or poor, old or young, bright or not-so-bright, well-read or poorly-read? The mystery of targeting my market confused me.

From where did the need to put one another in neat little boxes come? Like Campbell's soup cans, we all have labels.

Recently I had the joy of standing in front of a window in the maternity ward of a hospital. Little bassinets were all lined up in neat rows filled with wonderful little flannel-wrapped bundles. Each one within pounds of the other. They slept peacefully. Little hats warmed their heads. Parties had been held in their honor, a room awaited them someplace. Some rooms were newly painted in pink or blue or green or yellow. Those little bundles were so much alike. The art teacher in me made me compare them to a box of new crayons. They were all lined in a row. They were all alike. They were all new. They were all perfect. And, they were all waiting to be taken from their little box like bassinets. There were a few subtle differences. While some were light skinned, others were a medium skin tone. Some had blue eyes, some had brown, some green and some were a little hard to determine. So many similarities. Isn't it strange then that we dwell on small differences as life begins? The unimportant becomes more important than the important. Within days, the bundles of joy go home. Some become mommy's little darling, others become daddy's little helper. Some are greeted by two or three just-a-bit older siblings, and some go home as Number One. Life begins.

Some of those flannel bundles are always special. They become special to everyone, their teachers, their schoolmates, even Grandpa. While others are just another kid. Like the crayons, some get broken, divided, used, left alone, old, not liked or never really needed.

Our differences become society's curse. Schools work for conformity with standardized tests, competitions, and IQ scores. Words like bright, dull, special needs, chapters, subjects, tests, true-false, fill in the blanks, name in the upper right corner, to be written on white paper, 250 words, all become terms used over and over by the very people who were once upon a time wrapped in flannel bundles themselves. It is their turn to mold the crayons.

Someone had it done to them. It's time to do it to others.

The more I wrote, I found that I couldn't "target my market." When asked about my market, I am often questioned. "Well, for whom do you write?" I find myself searching for the correct answer. Early in my writing career, I had a book review and a book signing. A woman in the group finally answered that question for me.

"Her books are about life." she stated boldly.

"How I wanted to thank that woman. Silently, I have carried her observation with me. She got it. Even without its label, she got it! Life, that wondrous thing that happens from day to day while we think we are planning for it.

Those wonders wrapped in those little flannel bundles, cry out to be heard. It's troublesome trying to be liked, fitting in, working to be perfect, satisfying everyone and oneself at the same time. Television offers many views; society is filled with opinions.

As this thing called life goes into action, its quickness is alarming. Time gets short, we run to do things, we jump to do others, we grab hurriedly at things to sustain us, yet all the time we have had to fight hard to define ourselves. The crayon box, like the bassinet, is long gone. Half-read mysteries, historical journals, science fiction, novels, old philosophy books and fictional romances, sit collecting dust on shelves, bed stands and tables.

When is there time in life "to target your market?"

The next time you meet someone who asks, "And what do you do?" Respond loudly and clearly, "I live an exciting, happy, peaceful life, one day at a time putting one foot in front of the other. I work to love abundantly, to listen carefully, to rest peacefully and to pray to the Lord our God fervently and frequently.

Into each day will fall some rain, some sadness, some worry, some beauty, some loneliness, some snow, some joy, some laughter, some wonder and some mystery. Doors will shut, windows will open, good-byes will be said, hellos exchanged, farewells will bring sorrow and greetings will bring newness. All, however, will lead us to our destination, a destination so large and wonderful it will make that one flannel bundle of joy into a wondrous golden package of unspoken joy and elegance. We will be home. Life, as we knew it, will be over. Finally we can live life in the wonder of Heaven with our Lord beside us as He always was, but we were too busy to notice because we were trying to "target our market."

SIDNEY

SIDNEY WAS a tall, lanky teenager. His arms and legs were like tubes of rubber. He worked hard to adjust to his new adolescent body. From the first time he walked into my art room, I knew that he needed space, about double the space of his peers. He just couldn't resist poking and touching everything around him.

If we were to spend an hour of art class in peace, I had to find a place for Sidney that gave him the room to shake, rattle and roll as he painted and drew or glued and pasted. The idea worked. He loved his very own six-foot table in the back of the room. He could spread out in a space that was all his. He felt special.

Thirty-five years later, while I was a patient in a local hospital, one evening I took a turn for the worse. The young doctors on duty at 11:00 P.M. decided I would be more comfortable in intensive care.

"Let's call Transportation and have Mrs. Whitmer transported to ICU," one young doctor stated.

"Sounds good to me," the other replied.

As I glanced toward the door, in walked Sidney. It was my Sidney from long ago. He was no longer a long-legged adolescent. He entered the room pulling his black-leather gurney behind him. Immediately, we recognized one another. His marvelous smile showed a row of brilliant white teeth. He was glad to see me.

He never stopped talking as he loaded me onto his gurney, "Oh, Mrs. Whitmer, I'm so excited that I get to take you for your "last ride." I always wanted to thank you for treating me so special during my eighth-grade year in junior high school. I got into more fights, yet, never in your class. You gave me room to stretch out. In all the other classrooms, we sat so close together even our elbows bumped one another." Some place along the way I discovered that Sidney was the fourth child of nine children. They lived in a two-bedroom house.

As our trip to the ICU with Sidney at the helm began, he talked and talked non-stop. "Boy, I get to drive you to ICU, your last stop in the hospital." Every other phrase seemed to contain the word "last." He had me all but buried. He was to be the last of all those students to say good-bye.

He pulled and pushed the gurney with pride. However, the gurney had trouble cooperating. It had a bad wheel. It was old and overworked. As the gurney bumped the left side of the corridor. Sidney gave it a jerk! It then wobbled, changed directions, and smacked into the opposite wall. My husband walked along behind us. He tried to stay calm. While it was a very long and bumpy ride, we did make it to the ICU.

Once I was settled in ICU, Jerry laughed a little laugh and said, "Well, we learned one thing for sure on the way here. If you were able to survive the ride getting here, it's obvious you don't need to be here." We had a good laugh.

We watched as Sidney left the ICU, a big smile on his face. His last words along with a wet kiss were, "Don't worry Mrs. Whitmer, you're going to love heaven! God's going to be good to you for all the good things you've did for us kids. I hated art until I got you as my teacher. You had me design my dream home. I put a master bedroom in it with a big round bed and circular bathtub. I have those plans in my closet to this day and I still dream of building that house someday. You rest now. You're a good little woman."

I slept well that night knowing I had touched one wonderful young person when he most needed me. It takes years to realize the rewards of teaching. You never know the impact of our influence on children. And, the exchange is also true. Children affect our lives too.

"Giving away love is easy
Giving away a smile is even easier."

AUTHOR

SLEEPY TIME

THE FIRST night in a regular room after being in ICU
several weeks was a disaster. Sometime in the middle
of the night, I fell out of bed. No one had remembered
to put up the sides of the hospital bed. I was always safe
and secure in ICU. I knew nothing going on around me,
but I do remember feeling as though I was in a baby's
crib. Faces looked down at me.

I awoke with a jolt. For a moment, I could not remember
where I was. Something was cold and wet. My head
was between an opening at the bottom of the IV pole.
Hanging from the pole was a bag of something. Its' line

hung freely. Its' contents dripped on me. My "one size fits all" hospital gown was soaked. The only light from the hall was a thin gray shadow.

It took me a few minutes to realize that I was on the floor. The IV needle was no longer in my arm. My head was caught in one of the openings in the bottom of the IV pole. I wanted to ring for the nurse, yet I couldn't. The light button was tied to the bed. It was out of my reach.

I yelled "yoo hoo" several times, but I got no reply. Hospital night shifts are skimpy and over worked. I decided to be still and help would eventually come. Surely the lady who scrubbed the floor in the morning, with her big ugly mop, would find me.

I dozed off I'm not sure how long I was asleep. Suddenly, all the lights were on in the room. Someone had come to my aid. When that someone walked into the room, she yelled, "Look what you've done! Shame on you! You were not supposed to get out of your bed." We both knew how I ended up on the floor!

She helped me up, dried me off, reset the IV, and gave me a dry nightgown. She yanked the bed rails. Up they went. "Now stay in there," she ordered.

"I'm going to have my aid sit with you so you don't do anything like this again," she scolded. In walked a tank of a woman. She pulled the one decent chair in the room up to my bed, slid back into it, and got very comfortable. She then propped her size 12 feet on top of my bed.

She was to be my guardian. After all the excitement, it was hard to sleep. My head hurt where it had been pinched in the holes of the iv pole. I tried to be very still. Suddenly, with no warning, it sounded as though the pig from Green Acres was in my room. A big inhale from my gigantic guardian produced a rumbling, loud exhale. Gasping, grunting, with a ripple of snorting sounds ended her concerto. Soft to loud, in, out, her heavy throat muscles gurgled and rumbled.

I was supposed to sleep. She was there to care for me. Somehow none of it seemed right. I sat up. There she was, fast asleep. I pinched the toe of her huge sneaker. She was hard to awaken. She jerked a little. For a moment she forgot where she was. Her mouth was dry. "What, where, oh dear," she mouthed. "I need a glass of water."

She looked me in the eye and seemed to remember where she was and what she was doing there. I politely asked her to leave. There was no hassle. She pulled her heavy body from the fake leather chair and left. She left rubbing her eyes. Her sneakers squeaked on the well waxed floor. The last I heard from her was a big loud yawn. I lay back, thanked God I was in a clean, dry bed, with the sides up where they should have been all the time. Sleep finally came to me. Morning arrived. There never was any mention of the incident. You, my readers, are the first to hear about it. Why? I guess it's because I didn't want to make any trouble. I needed those people. Today I know better.

Today, I could pick her from a police lineup. She had sawed off short yellow hair along with a heavy accent and a "care not" attitude. Oh, well, all was safe and sound. Morning did come, and brought with it a new day would bring with new adventures.

"Only God knows the tomorrows of our lives."

AUTHOR

SEVEN COLORS OF HAIR

Is THERE any profession better than teaching? Never. And, teaching art is the best of any other subjects. Art is beauty. Art is from the inside. Art does not make the usual demands that other subjects do. Slow readers aren't exposed or embarrassed. There are no "secret" groups of readers named red birds, blue birds and crows to sort and separate the good from the mediocre and the dull. Equality reigns.

Children came to my classroom, sometimes sad, loud and annoyed from earlier classes encountered in their school day. They came alive knowing they could be who they were. They could get up and walk around, get a clean brush, new paint and clean water. They sat on stools, and were free to move about, exchange, borrow and watch others solve problems in their individual ways. There were no absolutes as there were in math or science. There were many solutions to every problem. Red or green, yellow or purple, blue or orange. Freedom was what it was all about.

My junior high curriculum program encouraged teaching things that a child could carry through life. We tried not to teach fancy tricks or difficult techniques. Ours was a program designed to reverse the usual notion that drawing realistically, or developing life long "artists" was all art class was about. Art was a time to learn, to look, to see. Art was a time to tell in picture form using color, imagination, texture and line of the world as he or she saw it. Clay and plaster, wood and wire allowed them to work three-dimensionally. Solid forms took shape. Positive and negative shapes took form sometimes by plan, sometimes by accident.

After my summer break from teaching, I could hardly wait to get to my art room. It was rectangular in shape with windows along one long side. Nice shelves and roomy cupboards along with a glass eight-foot showcase lined the opposite wall. A blackboard, bulletin boards, a huge paper cutter and my desk ran across the room front. The back was all bulletin boards, shelving, more cupboards and a sink the size of a bathtub — a shallow white, porcelain tub with four faucets evenly spaced over it.

It was such fun preparing for the first September day of school. I unrolled the American flag, placed it in its holder. I then decorated and prepared mini-stations and materials. Jars of paint were unpacked, large reams of paper were opened and stored for later use. Supplies had to last the entire year. We were careful not to waste anything in fear that we would run out of materials by January or February. Having no white paint or yellow paper could cause a near disaster. It was a little like how we hope our lives won't outlive our savings! Art teachers work hard to balance the materials with the length of the school year. It was okay to have empty cupboards in June, not in December!

Early each year I liked teaching interesting things about color. Primary, secondary, tertiary, analogous was an entire new vocabulary for exciting new seventh and eighth graders. A new world opened before their very eyes.

When I was 26, my hair had started to turn gray. My Mother hated my gray hair. She had dyed her hair for years and thought that if I had gray hair first, her friends would realize she most probably had gray hair too. She was annoyed that I refused to color my gray hair. Then one day in early June, my hairdresser made the remark, "As fast as your hair is graying, you're going to look like your husband's mother before you are 40."

Jerry's Mother was a lovely woman, yet I didn't want to look like her at 27 years old. And so, on one beautiful summer day, I weakened. Elizabeth, my hairdresser, wearing discolored, high yellow, rubber gloves, mixed a concoction in a large stained plastic cup. She painted my entire head with the goo that was the consistency of hot fudge. At the hairline, she put a coating of Vaseline. I sat for an hour with a pink plastic shower cap on my head. It covered the goo and kept it from running down my neck or cheeks or forehead. A little yellow oven timer finally dinged. My time was up. It was time for the grand uncovering.

Soap, shampoo, vinegar, hot water, cold water all were needed to break down the chemicals that had covered my scalp for an hour. The Vaseline had done its job in some areas while dark brown areas appeared where the Vaseline wasn't applied thickly enough. Elizabeth used Bab-o cleanser to scrub away the residual around my hairline. It turned red from scrubbing. I exited the beauty parlor a new person. Mother would be happy. She would look young again.

Most of my "dark summer hair" days were spent sitting in the sun, swimming in a chlorinated pool and doing the things that a summer in Ohio included. As the leaves began to turn their beautiful colors, I was refreshed and ready for a new school year. One day, as I sat at one of the large art tables, the children gathered around me in order that I could demonstrate the magic of color. Red would look redder if it was surrounded by green. Orange jumped out at you when placed near any shade or tint of blue. Wow! Blue even turned green if a spot of yellow were mixed into it. Red could easily become pink with a little white added to it.

The children moved in close to me. I could smell their perspiration, see crystal beads of sweat on their upper lips. Some had had gym before art. They had refused to take showers. The water and steam made their hair all "nappy" they told me. The heat of that late summer afternoon had made the few who knew to wear deodorant fail. Their warm bodies touched each other and also touched me. On my right stood Ronnie. He needed to blow his nose. His breathing warmed the lobes of my ears. In, out, there was a little whistle sound because of his stuffed up nose.

As I delighted them with my secrets about color, I worked to get them to perceive color in their world. What colors surrounded them? What colors were they? We talked about dark and light colors. Our skin tones were examined. Tans of all shades. They hated always having a box of crayons with "flesh" on the wrapper. It was never their skin color.

Just when things were at their very best, Ronnie broke the mesmerized silence of the warm-bodied, well-behaved group.

"You know what, Miz. Whitmer?" Ronnie asked. "You've got seven colors of hair."

"I do?" I responded. "What seven colors do you see?"

"Well, let's see" replied a challenged Ronnie. " I see black, brown, red, white, green, yellow green and rusty orange."

My color lesson ended. The summer sun, the chlorine in the pool, and my daily shampoo had turned my newly colored hair into "a head of many colors." Why hadn't I seen it? Why hadn't Elizabeth told me about the dangers of not protecting my newly colored hair? Today, the process has changed drastically since those mid 1960's, but not enough to ever allow me to go through the experience again.

Everyone around the table wanted to examine Ronnie's "find." I bent my head down as they picked through it. "Here's a red one," "Oh, look this has got to be the greenest one." "Well, I just found a beautiful white one." They were polite and fascinated. I'm not sure what I was.

I looked up to find the Principal standing with two officious looking men from the school board. They had come to visit my classroom. They stood watching my lesson on color as it disintegrated to a group of kids going through my hair as though they were trying to see who could find the most lice or fleas. It must have been a wonderful sight!

Ronnie was quick to realize what was happening and even quicker to step up to explain what had happened.

We all had a good laugh. After school, I walked to my car late that September afternoon knowing one thing for sure, Elizabeth was never going to get another chance to attempt to keep me "younger than springtime." My hair turned gray quickly. Elizabeth was right. Because of it, I am frequently mistaken for Jerry's Mother. I was not up to another "head of many colors." Out of the mouth of Ronnie came the truth. My friends, my family, never said a word. While teaching those sweet, kind, brilliant young children how to look, to see, and to really examine, they saw the truth. And, they were brave and innocent enough to speak it. My happiest days remain those days in that wonderful art room. With the doors closed, my 30 plus or minus a few students and I were safe and happy. We were free with the truth. Last week I saw Ronnie for the first time in 40 years. He looked into my face with a blank stare. Today he is a grown man. When I spoke to him, he softened. He remembered me from my voice, not my face or head of gray hair. Teaching is good no matter the color of your hair.

"Stories of who we were are the gifts
of who we are this day."

AUTHOR

"Hope is the thing with feathers

that perches on the soul."

EMILY DICKINSON

THE CENTURIES OF
OUR LIVES

PEOPLE OFTEN want to divide their lives into neat sec-
tions-like cutting a pie into exact pieces-all equal in
shape and size. Recently, I received a letter from a wonderful Jesuit priest. His letters have been a major source
of inspiration in my life, and have helped me stay headed
in the right direction. He writes about thoughts and feelings. At age 80 he claims it to be at the best time in his
life. Wow!

Our society dwells on youth. How can he say he's "happier than he has ever been?" That statement would confuse most people. The decades of our life are measured in a variety of ways. Father Gene's letter made me think all week about my own life. What decade of my life was best? Which one was better than another was?

Strange, now that I have tried to sort it all out, I've come to one simple conclusion. The teen years were not sweet. The sweet sixteen-year-old that I appeared to be on the outside was not there. Teenagers are targeted. They represent a part of youth that has such negative connotations. Once I started teaching, I realized that much of the doom I dreaded at that age came from the outside. There always seemed to be an attitude of "teenagers just don't know much, they don't measure up."

In actuality, teenagers are brilliant in the honest way they view their world and their place in it. My junior high teaching days gave me an appreciation and an understanding for that decade of time spent growing in so many ways. What I realize now is that teenagers just simply need to be heard and we need to respond to them. I liked that decade of my life better once I was able to look back on it. Teaching teenagers taught me about the treasures they had hidden deep within.

In our society, we sometimes think, that the 20's were the best decade of our lives. Good health, bodies at their best, nice relationships with people of the opposite sex, new freedoms, all blended to make it the dream of the part of our life that would last forever. Were these the best years of our life? I think not. The kind of person I am, I have discovered, needed more peace, more security, and more stability, than those years offered. And, while I am a process person in most things I do, the process of settling into life that was expected of me at that time was disheartening. Twenty meant so much new. New relationships, new environment, new positions, new living conditions, new friends and new places. I learned much about myself during my 20's. While it was a time of moving forward, it was also a big time for reflection on what had gone before it. With each decade came the reality that we really know so little about everything. My own areas of specialty seemed weak. Learning became important. The more I learned, the more I wanted to learn. Like the branches of a big lovely oak, my branches took shape. These were years when I realized I was capable of all sorts of things. Staying focused at the same time as exploring the new was work.

Our 30's seem to be a settling-in time. The family unit as we know it is somehow at its best. Grandpa and Grandma have settled in. Children become helpful. Life felt good. Yet, my own 30's slipped by so quickly that it all seems like a blur. I was in them one day and out of them the next. My Mother's heart gave way and ended her cheerful little life. Hard work was the expected. Little leisure time was left at the end of long full days.

Being 40 was fun. It was a time of respecting one another; growth seems at its peak. And, 50 seemed far away. The speed of it all leveled off. The uncertain became less. Directions and perceptions seem hard-lined. Uncertainty grew less. Life was more comfortable. Even with serious illness at 42, I felt no fear or disappointment. It was a hopeful decade. What was to be, was. My day-at-a-time philosophy took shape. Was it the best decade of my life? I'm not sure. So far, each has been exciting, fun-filled; each filled with its own magic.

In retrospect, the 40's really flew by, However, it's remarkable how much the 50's flew by even faster. With the newness of real years under our belts, we become surer, more real, softer edged.

As we grow older, people occasionally will ask what we think the best decade is in the aging process. The best? I find myself never able to quite put my finger on it. I keep debating with myself-good, better, best? Is there that comparison in the aging process? Each holds its own place in time; each accumulation of years builds wisdom, love, experiences and depth. In each are changes that bring with them their own discoveries. There are good and not so good in each. Perhaps the best is tomorrow. Maybe Father Gene is right, being 80 will be the best!

"People heal hearts by using theirs."

AUTHOR UNKNOWN

2005

Today is the first day of a New Year. The gray of the day does not bother me. Inside, my day is a bright and contented day in 2005. We wonder what it will bring. Where will it take us? The wondering of life can get us in trouble. Wondering leads to questioning. Questioning brings on anxiety. Anxiety keeps us from moving forward with real joy. Anxiety brings with it "what ifs." The "what-ifs" have always and will always be part of life. It's not in the plan for us to know the parts of the whole. Yet, we seem to want to know. We think that knowing will make us feel better. Being better people is built into being human. It takes work to allow the future to be open-ended and in the hands of someone greater than we. "I hope to begin 2005 by releasing myself from the desire to control the tomorrow of my life."

Life is good. Life gets better. Life is lovely. Life is real. Life is all there is right now.. Life goes on and on. Life holds hope. Life is just a little four-letter word. Life holds surprises. Life waits until death. Life contains disappointments. Life is full if we want it to be. Life is never boring. Life is a process. Life unfolds in an orderly fashion. Start today to have LIFE!

"It is easier to accept today because we have memories of yesterday."

AUTHOR

HER HAT CAUGHT
ON FIRE

CAROL WAS my best friend. Oh, how we loved one
another. If she wasn't going to church, I didn't want
to go to it either. If she wasn't at school, the day was
a waste. We laughed at the silliest of things. We spent
hours talking and laughing.

Our best laughter seemed always to be in church. One
day we were saying the Stations of the Cross. The
Stations are the story of Christ's last hours on earth.
There are 14 Stations. Churches usually have them hung

between the colored glass windows along the sides of the church. We had seven of them evenly distributed on each side of the church. They were lovely relief sculptures made of plaster and rubbed to patina-like finish. They were about three feet tall and two feet wide.

At each Station, we would stop to say the Station represented by Christ on His way to His Crucifixion. At each stop we would kneel, pray, meditate and contemplate the highly brutal, sad way Christ died. The Stations of the Cross were especially solemn and profound.

The Station I felt worst about was the crowning of thorns. To this day, roses always remind me of that crown of thorns put on Christ's head. How it must have hurt! We all know how much just one thorn feels if accidentally touched.

We were quiet as we worked through the stations; pious sixth graders were we. Easter was near. We were holy little girls with our hands in the prayer position. It was the season of Lent. The season when all the fun things in life were considered bad. We gave up candy, going to movies, cake, the list went on and on. The only thing to do was to go to church, whisper a little and laugh, quiet tiny laughs.

We were about half way down the aisle, kneeling in front of the Seventh Station when something caught our eyes. We looked up to the front of the church. A little, old lady was lighting a candle in a red glass votive container. As she bent to put the wick on the tray under the candles so someone else might use it, the feathers across the complete front of her oversized black hat caught fire.

In horror, I pointed to what I saw. I was paralyzed not knowing what to do. Carol was a quick thinker. She jumped up from her kneeling position on the cold marble floor, ran to the woman, pulled out the long hatpin with the bright gold ball on the end which held the hat on the woman's head and threw the hat to the floor. She stomped out the fire. Carole's quickness confused the lady. She did not realize that the entire hat was seconds from going up in flames.

There was a terrible rumpus. The woman picked up the charred hat and hit Carole on the head. She cursed. She screamed. She chased after Carole. Poor Carole had to run to get away from her.

For us, the Stations were over. We sat outside. Carole was covered with soot and charcoal. She had tried to do the right thing and just look at what happened! We were hysterical after all the burnt feathers hit the floor. We never forgot the incident. It became our best story of all. As we told it, we laughed long before we even got to the part about the hat. We knew the ending.

As we left church with the Stations of the Cross unfinished, we just couldn't stop laughing.

As we walked down 6th Street, we came upon our favorite milkshake place, called B and B. Just the sight of the place made us drool for a chocolate shake. It was Lent. We reminded each other milkshakes were on the "No" list. Yet, seeing as we had saved that poor woman's life, we decided to set aside one of our Lenten promises. We had the best shake we had ever had. We never told anyone.

For years, I would imitate Carole jumping on that poor soul's hat and Carole would imitate me with my eyes as big as gumballs, my mouth hanging wide open and my finger pointing to what I couldn't believe I was seeing.

We acted out the "hat fire" scenario for our parents and anyone else who would laugh at our dramatic story of this fun day in church.

The milkshakes became one of our very special secrets. Oh, wasn't it fun to have a favorite, wonderful, fun, best friend? I miss my Carole. She died several years ago of cancer. She died never telling our secrets to anyone. I can hardly wait to get to Heaven so we can act out the event again. By then the story will surely be bigger and better. Childhood stories are like that!

WONDERS OF YOUTH

WHEN I was young, I would ask my Mother every day, "What day is this?" I had just discovered the mystery of the calendar. Her reply was always the same, "It's Monday, all day," she would say, or "it's Friday, all day." Every reply ended with, "all day."

I would study the calendar. It was fun finding which Monday or which Friday it was. Most of the calendar made sense except for the blocks under Monday or whatever days that were slashed in half from opposite corners. Two numbers were in one block. Those were the half-day about which Mother spoke when she replied "all day."

My childish brain couldn't figure what those half days were going to be like. What would happen to lunch? What time would it start to get dark? How long would we sleep on a half day? Would we awake to another breakfast or would it be time for dinner. Oh, how I worried and wondered! Strange that it never ever happened. I had struggled to make any sense out of it.

It was one of those confusing things adults said like, "Oh, there is a horse fly in the house!" How in the world did a horse get in the house and how could he fly with no wings?

When I was about six or seven years old, we stopped in a tiny town while on a little driving vacation. Mother looked from the window of our cozy tourist home room and said, "Boy, I'll bet they take the sidewalk in at night in this town." As I tried to drift off to sleep I had visions of people lifting up the concrete slabs. Where did they put them for the night? How heavy were they? That night I decided I finally had an answer to why sidewalks had cracks evenly distributed between each slab. It was because they were easier to take in at night. They folded on each crack.

I could hardly wait for morning to arrive. I wanted to watch the people unfold the cement slabs. The first thing I did after I awoke was run to the window. "Oh, I missed it," I said in disappointment.

"Missed what?" Mother asked.

"The laying of the sidewalk," I answered.

Mother and Daddy laughed. Oh, the wonders of youth!

"Nothing is ever too much to do for a child."

MARY VIRGINIA MERRICK
Founder of National
Christ Child Society, Inc.

GRACE

GRACE WAS kind. Grace was liked by everyone. She was very bright. She always had a good book that she was reading. She loved things either really big or things very small. She never had a mean thing to say about anyone or anything. Grace had a deep quietness within her.

Being with Grace was easy. She was a good listener. She was sincere in wanting to know about the lives of her friends. Her life was calm, orderly and uncluttered.

Her cancer disappointed her. Yet, she handled it with the same graciousness with which she lived her life. There was never a complaint. Like some strong soldier, she accepted treatment. Her bridge game got set on a back burner. Her golfing stopped. She never complained.

Her Fall funeral was peaceful. The church was still. The service was eloquent. Her sons spoke of the wonders of their mother. She was sad about not having grand-children. Yet, she delighted in the bright minds and independence of her three loving sons.

Her quiet self is difficult to forget. The hole in our hearts that she left behind seems never to get smaller. Her high school friends relived their joy of the years when they first met during their eloquent words of her eulogy.

Soft spoken, words tried to fill the emptiness of the simple chapel where no words seemed right. Grace was now gone from us, never again to be part of an evening of fun or an afternoon of sharing. We must wait patiently. We know perfectly well that we simple souls will be reunited. We will all walk hand in hand with our friend, Grace, and all the others who have gone before us in the sign of peace.

"In your heart your dreams await
the chance to fly, let them out."

Margaret Boyd

FRIENDS

Quiet the Night
Peaceful and warm
They sleep
One in a ball
The other long stretched tall.

One so large
And one so small
Each respects the other
That one is all girl and
The other all boy makes no matter.

One is gray
The other is red
Oval are their heads
Long their tails
With whiskers as strong as nails.

Life they enjoy
Trust is all they know
One follows the other
Like sister and brother
Like friends forever.

Filled with personality
One so loud
One so quiet
Never a hassle
Nor never a tassel.

One runs full speed
The other tiptoes
One needs a weekly bath
The other grooms himself
For, one is a dog; the other a cat.

They each have their own favorite places
To eat, to sleep
To rest, to linger and to creep
To look, to stare
A cool breeze to share.

With never a word
Or sharing of food
They get what they want
Even for lunch
From early morning to the quiet of night
They are a delight.

We marvel at their wonder
They were born to slumber
While quiet the night
They see with little light
Good night

Almond eyes shine brightly
One has tiny upstanding ears
The other's are long and shaggy
Yet, two things are clear
They are always so near and dear.

*"Love for life is as easy as you
make it."*

AUTHOR

DOROTHY

ONCE YOU are a cancer patient, you search for the how, the what, the when, and the why. I have searched for over 25 years. Oh, not a daily search, or a research kind of search. I mean that, every now and again I wonder. Something will click. When I was in high school, I ate lunch with seven other female classmates at a long rectangular table. I sat at one end of the table. Connie was always on my right. Carole to my left. Connie died at 52 of cancer, Carole at 57. I was diagnosed with cancer at 42. I don't know the stories of the other four at that same table. I wonder.

I saw Dorothy today. Her smile was just as I remembered it. We were college roommates in 1958. In the summer, we worked together as waitresses in Lake Placid, New York. We were both art majors. We took almost all the same courses.

Our favorite professor in the School of Art taught ceramics. Around us were clay glazes and kilns, both large and small. The facility was poorly ventilated. We experimented with different ways to arrive at a variety of fired surfaces. Mothballs were sometimes added just when the kiln reached its highest temperature. We found the mothballs produced a lovely lustrous surface.

Dorothy stayed on to work on a Master's degree in enameling with our favorite professor. We called him

Mory. He wasn't much older than we were. Mory died four years ago from a rare stomach cancer.

Today when Dorothy spoke, she eloquently described her cancer and all the treatments her doctor is using to fight

The War

A Battle

Terminal

The Big C

The Epidemic

The Enemy

Thousands lie in bed this night pouring over the same thoughts. Where did we go wrong? What causes some of the strange similarities? I have no answers. Far brighter minds than mine are asking far more intelligent questions. Yet, I wonder, along with eight million other people.

Will we live to see the end to it all? Will we find the enemy? Will terminal go back to being the word meaning what it once did? Will The Big C ever be erased from our vocabulary? Will someone ever admit that this very day we are in the midst of a real epidemic? Then and only then will we be able to

Stop the War!

Cease the Battle!

End the Terminal Disease!

Stomp Out The Big C!

Look back at what was an Epidemic!

And, Vaguely Remember the Enemy.

The Enemy named Cancer.

DAY BY DAY

MY TALKS began quietly enough, one led to another. Day by day, week by week, and year by year. The more I knew, the more I realized how little I really knew.

Experience after experience grew into a story of life. Could there be meaning in each day if my memory would sort it all out for the good of others? What else really matters when you analyze it all? Things, places, clutter, money, who really cares? The only constants in it all are relationships with one another and with God. We spin our wheels, repeat the same mistakes, struggle to please, and satisfy our own egos, all the time wondering why? What's it all about? It is about quiet, peace and calm.

> *Silence the storms of your life.*
> *Step aside; don't let life get overwhelming.*
> *Wipe the tears of trouble from your eyes.*
> *Scrub the corners of your heart.*
> *Make room in your heart for more love.*
> *Identify misplaced treasures.*
> *Surround yourself with good.*
> *Realize the right way.*
> *Stay on the right path.*
> *Take an inventory of your life often.*

Have you strayed from your path? How easy it is to get whisked away into troubled waters. Just one small word, one little thought, one tiny action can take us from our smooth journey to a bumpy rough road. Ruts grab us. Our tires sink down deeper. We lose sight. How easily it all can happen. Stop and listen. Reach to be saved from yourself. Be open and ready for the good in your life. Sing and dance. Laugh and linger. The peace for which we all yearn will be yours when you least expect it. Your prayer will be answered. Celebrate!

LEARNING TO TRUST

A T 5:30 A.M. in the hospital, a light goes on in the room. A perfect stranger announces that she is there to draw blood. With sleepy eyes and outstretched arms, the process begins. Is that trust? I believe it is. Yet, our world pours "horror" stories upon us hours and hours each day that tell of the bad in people. These stories are repeated over and over again. They tear away our trust. We gradually lose our love for one another because of the actions of such a very few. Be your own person. Absorb the good things of life. Turn off the over repeated stories of ugliness. Reach out for the positive, good things that happen every day. Move away from being common. It takes nothing but commitment and determination. Be the special creature you were born to be.

"Keep your heart a place where dreams can grow."

AUTHOR

CAREER

As a young healthy teacher of art in a junior high school, I saw 150 children a day each for forty-five minutes. That amounts to 700 children a week. After a semester break, a new group of 700 students greeted me. To this day, nearly 30 years later, I still have my grade books and my lesson plan folders. As I glance down the columns of names, wonderful smiling faces of children flash through my mind. The things they said, the places they sat, the questions they asked, and the art they produced, I remember the details vividly. Why? I'm not sure.

I just loved teaching and I loved every single child I ever taught.

Since I started writing, some wonderful things have happened. Old students, now grown adults, find my books in all sorts of places and have written to me. My mailbox, once filled with mostly junk mail, now has delightful surprises in it. Those lovely little souls have grown into wonderful adults. How did it happen? Adults walk up to me, in the grocery store or in a museum or a restaurant. They are taller than I am; some are bald, some are sad, even broken, from lives that have not gone as they had hoped. Yet, they stand before me. I am Mrs. Whitmer to them.

I saw Carolyn just recently. Only yesterday, she was a ball of energy, a cheerleader who could run across the gym floor and touch the back of her head with the bottoms of her cleanly polished gym shoes. Her cartwheels were round, toes pointed and perfect. She could cover the gym floor from end to end in quick precision. White teeth shone, she clapped in rhythm and used her pom-poms to cheer with her admiring audience.

Last night she stood before me. As we spoke, she politely called me, "Mrs. Whitmer." I noticed she called my husband Jerry. I marveled as he ever so respectfully greeted her with "Hello, Judge Casey." Today, little

Carolyn Casey is a dignified, refined, bright judge. All evening, I was "Mrs. Whitmer" to her. She was and will always be Carolyn to me. While some things change, a few never do. Gone are her navy blue pleated cheerleading skirt and the wonderful wool sweater with the big felt letter "C" on its back, which stood for Central. She now dons a black robe every day. She stands tall. The court respects her presence and her words of wisdom. No one ever told me those little twelve and thirteen-year olds were going to grow into beautiful, bright, handsome, outstanding, mannerly adults. Wow!

All the way home I thought of Carolyn and what a magnificent adult she had become. I asked Jerry why he insisted on calling my little Carolyn, Judge Casey?

"Because she is." His eyes were wide with wonder and praise and respect.

Just as she will always be Carolyn to me, I will be Mrs. Whitmer to her. What we do in life sometimes sticks with us forever!

"Our memories stick with us forever."

AUTHOR

BATTLE WITH
THE BOLT

IN THE house where we lived when I was a child, there was right in the center of the garage floor where you would least expect it, a three-inch bolt that stuck up two inches from the garage floor. In the summer, we were sure to go to bed at night with stubbed, sore, black-and-blue toes. As often as we were reminded to "watch the bolt," it was always there. Sometimes though, it seemed to move from place to place. My toes hurt now just remembering the "battle of the bolt."

Perhaps it represented what was to be part of life. Each step we take we must be careful for there are "bolts" along the path of life. They hinder our progress. Like the bolt in the garage floor as a child today they surround us. They are a part of our daily lives. We can somehow bump into things that make no sense in our real journey. Why is it that so often we realize them after the fact? We knew, we had learned to move away, yet we were tempted. Yes, we know of things like the "bolt in the garage floor," yet we stumbled on them daily.

Why is it that we continue to do the same thing expecting different results? New results will only happen if new behaviors are developed. Let us not get to Heaven with bruised toes.

"Prayer is our talk with our Lord.
Call out and be specific. Then, listen
carefully for the whispered answer."

AUTHOR

AND PLASTIC MADE
THE SCENE

IT WAS a new wonderful thing. Mother was delighted. It would make our lives so much easier.

"Look, you can wash it off with a wet cloth! No washer, no ironing!" she announced one bright summer day. I was eight years old.

Out of a flat rectangular cardboard box, she lifted a new plastic tablecloth. It was creamy white with red cherries spread at random all over its surface. I thought it was ugly. Until this time, our tablecloths had always been made from cloth. They were usually sadly worn, old, highly valued Irish linen passed down to us from Grandmother Casey. We called her Bid, short for Bridget.

Mother spread the new plastic cloth on the kitchen table. She rubbed her hands across it trying to press down the heavily creased folds. Gone was the starched linen ironing smells. Bid's treasures were put to rest. I was sad.

What was this thing called plastic? It seemed oily, sticky, tacky, and smelly all at the same time. As I think back I realize my dislike for it was almost immediate. It had no redeeming qualities as far as I could see. Soon after the plastic tablecloth arrived, a plastic shower curtain, and a plastic apron were to follow. Gradually, the smell took over our little postwar bungalow. Oh, how I dreaded eating from that oily, stinky, new invention. Finally, to appease me, Mother would put an open linen napkin at my place at the table. That I was treated special annoyed my older sister. "Big sissy, spoiled brat," filled our evening meal conversation.

The shower curtain kept water off of the bathroom floor, yet it smelled of "that smell" and as the warm, sudsy water residue accumulated. It was slimy to the touch. Oh, how I hated it! However, the "miracle" of plastic's greatness broke one day when my Mother was ironing while she was wearing her plastic apron. At first, a dark sticky something rubbed from the iron onto Daddy's best shirt.

"What's wrong with the iron?" Mother wondered aloud. As she continued to iron, long melted strings of black goo covered the beautiful oxford cloth dress shirt.

Mother was disgusted, frustrated and confused by the iron that had been such a "wonderful iron for 21 years." What had happened to it to cause it to stick? Left-handed Mother, using an iron intended for a right-handed person, had awkwardly hit the hot iron on the "beauty of an apron." Each time she pulled the iron close to her, it hit the plastic apron. When the heat of the iron melted the "wonderful new invention," it stuck to the side and bottom of the iron just enough to carry a soft black gooey gob across the starched, lovely shirt.

The apron was ruined, as was the shirt. It had big burned holes across its front, almost like bullet holes. The iron had to go to the shoe repair shop where Mr. Wagner also fixed irons. The goo was insoluble and the one and only Sunday shirt was cut up for window cleaning rags, after the buttons were removed.

On that warm summer day in our house, plastic moved down the ladder of marvelous new inventions. Thank you, God.

To this day, I have an aversion to plastic. It has continued to be a fake, man-made thing that can save lives and do many good things, yet it fills our landfills, will not disintegrate, and has remained on my list of things that I dislike. Its texture, colors, and most of all, its smell, have continued to disgust that part of me that enjoys the beauty of the real world. How life can be changed with one small invention turned big. Today, we cannot even image a life without plastic. Yet, that doesn't mean we have to like it!

"Isn't the strength of the human spirit amazing?"

AUTHOR

GREEN PAPER

A FTER INTRODUCING a new art lesson to a large group of seventh graders, they got down to work. John was a little on the awkward side. As the youngest in his seventh-grade class, he struggled with his eye-hand coordination. I had planned the lesson to include the need for pasting one piece of eighteen by twenty-four inch colored paper to another the same size. The shapes cut from the top sheet left negative spaces. The top sheet glued to a lighter or darker plain sheet of paper made the negative cutout spaces become filled. They were no longer negative shapes. The assignment was that the students were to design their names using a variety of processes that would express things about them. Taller children used tall letters; short, round children made their letters low to the guidelines with flattened, full shapes near the bottom. Children who liked to run slanted their letters to the right, while kids who like to walk slowly made their letters lean to the left. The colors they selected represented their personality. Red, for instance, might suggest someone with a quick temper while blue was someone who might be quiet or maybe a little sad. They seemed to always find a reason for one color over another because we had discussed the depth of the meaning of color.

As they worked, I passed out "The All-American Paste," one jar to each table. I announced to each table of four, "Here's your paste for when you need to paste the two pages together." I might add that Elmer's Glue was just new on the market, but it was too expensive for the school system to supply so, the paste had to do the job. Do you remember it? It had a delicious smell; we used tongue depressors to scoop it out of the jars. Every so often, and quite predictably, someone would eat some. It never failed. I would have to say, "Now, don't eat your paste," more than once a day!

Nine tables had paste. I had announced it to all thirty-some children. Not three minutes after I had distributed a jar and tongue depressor to every single one of my little angels, up came John.

"How can I get this, the Kelly Green paper with the letters JOHN cut from it, to stick to this the black sheet of paper?" he asked innocently. Tired and a bit irritated that I had just moments before looked him in the eye and put the paste smack dab in front of him, I sarcastically responded, "You lick it." This is where I get ashamed of myself. My heart flutters even today and I get embarrassed knowing I did something so terrible and humiliating. He returned to his seat and began licking the 18x24 piece of bright green paper. It was inexpensive paper, absorbent, like a blotter. He licked and he licked. The other children began poking one another and laughing. Some watched in fascination.

John's lips and tongue turned green-a nice moss-like green covered his smooth soft skin around his rosy cheeks. Whatever had I done? And more important, how was I going to tell him I was only joking? It was a sad, sorry few minutes. He licked and he licked and finally, after every spot was covered, he lined up the edges of the background paper carefully and rubbed it together as we once did postage stamps on envelopes. The top sheet fell off. He licked some more. It fell off again. The room got unnaturally quiet. Everyone was watching in awe. Whatever had I done? How was I going to get out of the situation?

Gently, I approached him and as nicely as I could I asked, "John, why don't you use the paste?" He looked at me wide-eyed and confused. "Why did you tell me to lick it?" His innocence made me want to cry. It makes me want to cry this very minute, all these years later.

I apologized for my blunder, loud enough for the class to hear. I walked home that night, head down. I was sorry for what had happened that day. As John left the room, his green lips were turned up, he was polite. He said goodbye. Shortly after he had gone to the bathroom, he reappeared at my classroom door. "Look," he said proudly as he stood with his mouth wide open, "My mouth looks like I'm a frog inside." There was no malice, there were no tears. There was only my heavy, sad heart. Sarcasm is a terrible form of humor. Children just do not understand it. In a way, it is very mean spirited.

Forty years later, a tall and handsome grown man walked up to me at a special black-tie event. He stood in front of me and opened his mouth where perfect white teeth were in two neat rows. He proudly announced, "LOOK, I'm not green anymore. Do you remember me?"

All that wonderful person will ever remember of his junior high art class and his art teacher will be, "You're the teacher who made me lick that huge, yucky green paper in seventh grade." Wow! That was a day that has lived to haunt me.

Over the years as our paths have crossed, I have apologized. Yet I am sorry it happened. The wrongs we innocently commit seldom are intended at the time. Our busy world gets in the way of a gentle spirit.

"Let us not replace wisdom with cleverness."

E. F. SCHUMACHER
Small is Beautiful

A TRIP TO THE DRUGSTORE

A S AN education major, I was required by the University to take a speech course. The course consisted of the usual things taught in a basic, fundamental course in speech. The course included things that required us to prepare and deliver an assortment of assignments in front of the class. Our out-of-class work included visits with speech therapists in a variety of schools, learning the structure and anatomy of the mouth, how words were formed, and the ability to identify speech impediments. A "lateral s," for example, is the sound of the letter "s" over the sides of the tongue, while expelling air with the tongue on the roof of the mouth, thus making a sound like a train stopping at a station rather than an "s" like a hissing snake makes.

We all had to learn these impediments in speech patterns in order that we could identify them in children and refer the child to the speech therapist. One very important speech problem we had to learn was that of stuttering. We explored the whys, whens and wherefores of stuttering. I loved the drama of learning to stutter and I quickly became the best at it in the class. Often, stuttering children had trouble with the letter "m." For them, the words that began with or contained "m" were difficult and haunting. We were required to learn all of the "stutter's letters." My best was the letter "n." "Na,na,na,na," I'd have the class on the edges of their seats in apprehension of what was to follow. Was I trying to say "nurse" or "nice," or maybe even "never?"

One out-of-class assignment was to go into a store to speak with someone using our learned impediments in order that we could witness how it felt to have a speech problem. The goal of the assignment was to study the way people responded to our problem. Our professor wanted us to know first hand how a person with a speech problem felt living in a world of people who expected our speech patterns to be a particular, "accepted" way.

My particular assignment was to go to a drug store and ask the pharmacist for a jar of Noxzema. I had to take a classmate with me to witness that I had indeed completed the assignment.

The drugstore was on the corner of Main and Water Street in Kent, Ohio. It was a warm spring Saturday. I had practiced. After I got up the nerve to complete the assignment, I walked up to the counter.

"Na, na, na, nox, nox, nox, noxe, noxe," and, before I could get the "ma" syllable out, the wide-eyed, anxious pharmacist yelled as loud as he could, "NOXZEMA!" He had won the battle. He had found the word for me! He was jubilant. I was sad. I had wanted to get it out, all of it, by myself. He acted as though he had won some silly game. Everyone in the store looked at the two of us. My classmate ran from the store, her face red from holding in a burst of laughter. I found her sitting on the curb, bent over. I walked from the store with my little brown bag, holding its little blue jar of Noxzema.

I did, indeed, learn much that day. I learned that in this "expect perfection" world of ours, it is not easy to be the least bit imperfect. I shall never forget the look of apprehension and agony on the face of the pharmacist as he tried to help me spit out just one simple word, and I shall also never forget the faces of the other people in the drugstore. I was the center of attention, the reason for laughter and mimicry that spring day and I didn't like the feeling.

As my teaching years passed, my heart always went out to the innocent stutterers. None of them went without my help. I did not want them to have to live a life experiencing what I had experienced for just a few moments as I tried to buy a simple jar of Noxzema. Today I laugh at the assignment and the memory of my classmate on the curb laughing. I do not, however, find anything funny in a handicap.

If ever you have the opportunity to talk with a former stutterer, learn from their early painful experiences. Those experiences for me were pretty profound. If the one word Noxzema caused the embarrassment it did that day, think how difficult a life with the smallest of imperfections could be!

What can we do to make a hard-edged world into a soft-edged place where we will together accept all our imperfections? Perhaps we need to stop for just one day and walk in the shoes of another. That little, yet brilliant speech class assignment truly taught me much. It opened my eyes and my wonderful roommate's eyes to the difficulty of others and how our world reacts to them. "There but for the grace of God go I."

"We must cry out that others may sing."

AUTHOR UNKNOWN

A SHOE IN THE LOCKER

GOING TO a hospital can be a traumatic experience. Going to a hospital in a strange new environment can be really traumatic. I now understand why people like to stay in their own communities when they get sick. Yet, sometimes this isn't possible. In my own case all those years ago, I had to go to Washington for treatment. Experimental drugs were my last hope. The Food and Drug Administration demanded double blind studies before it would give approval for the general use for people with cancer. And, the National Institutes of Health needed people to volunteer to take the drugs.

Clinical trials are required in order to eliminate the side effects of the new drugs. The trials are labeled phase one, phase two and on down the line. Often a drug isn't given the green light after phase one because of dangerous side effects.

When I walked into the hospital to the room to which I was assigned in the Clinical Center, Building 10, Floor 10, a very sick roommate greeted me. I had never seen anyone as sick as she.

The nurse turned down my bed and pointed to a locker and a rectangular drawer under it. That was where I was to put my things.

Overwhelmed by the newness of everything, I gradually tried to adjust. I sat on the edge of the bed a moment to take in all that surrounded me.

Slowly I took off my clothing and slipped into the hospital gown the nurse had left for me. Isn't it amazing how alike hospital gowns are year after year after year? "One size fits all," Not so. My, they are ugly!

Finally, I removed my shoes. I opened the rectangular drawer to put them away. In the drawer sat one worn sneaker. Just one. It was a sneaker of quality. It was for the right foot. I thought someone had forgotten to take it home.

Thinking that the person might still be in the hospital, I hurried to the nurses' station with the shoe in hand. I told the nurse where I found it. I was worried that the person to whom it belonged would be really sad to have left it behind. It looked like part of someone's favorite pair of sneakers. You know how we Americans are about our sneakers!

The nurse casually looked up at me from the desk, glanced at the shoe and without much emotion said. "Oh, that belonged to Jennifer, the young girl who had your room. She had her leg amputated. I guess she didn't need to take the shoe. She no longer had a right foot on which to wear it."

I stood frozen. The shoe had personality. It was all broken-in. It looked comfortable. The foot that once wore it was gone. Jennifer just left it behind as she did her leg and her foot. What must something like that be like?

Her cancer had been in the calf area of her leg. Getting rid of it meant getting rid of her leg to stop the spread of the disease. The study and the clinical trials were designed to see if the disease would spread if the tumor site were gone. Years later, it was determined that amputation really wasn't what they had hoped it would be.

Jennifer could have gone home with both sneakers and would do so today because of what was learned through that phase of that study. Courageous people like Jennifer took the chance of their lives. It meant more than just leaving a shoe behind for someone like me to find.

It meant an entirely new lifestyle. I was to meet Jennifer years later. She was happy. She had adjusted. Along with her shoe, she left behind her earlier self. Who knows what had worked? One of the experimental drugs or surgery? Was it the chemotherapy that followed her amputation? Was it the radiation she agreed to try? Was it prayer? Was it determination? God only knows. Whatever the case, she no longer needed the shoe that she left behind for me to find. She was able to say farewell to her leg and foot and thigh and calf and so much more with a smile on her face. She was alive after months of hard work, patience and a powerful amount of hope. All these years later, I wonder where life has taken her. Her shoe remains a beautiful reminder of the things we are forced to leave behind in order to move forward.

"In the absence of strife, a fertile future grows."

AUTHOR

A SPOONFUL OF
MEDICINE

DID YOU KNOW that some school buses are called
Bluebirds? Why would you call a big, yellow-orange
boxy school bus a Bluebird? Could the name come from
reading groups of long ago? Do you remember those
reading groups? Oh, how I would have loved to have
been a "bluebird!" I was always in the "redbird" group.
Teachers thought that we didn't know what those groups
meant, but we knew as well as we knew our names.
That handful of special "bluebirds" gathered around the

teacher on their little chairs. Oh, how she loved them! She loved hearing them read. Words flowed from their little mouths. There was no struggle; her face was calm and relaxed. The groups that followed brought a frown to her face. Her voice changed.

Memories of our school days surface as though they were yesterday. My grade school years were in Canton, Ohio. There were fifty-four of us in our class. Together we traveled all eight grades. Now, having taught some twenty years myself, I cannot, for the life of me, understand how those poor nuns taught fifty-four of us at one time with no help. We ranged from big to small, bright to dull, and, while a few were "bluebirds," there were also a few non-readers, and many in between.

Let me tell you one story of my days in third grade. Sister was young, we were younger. She was nervous; her nails were bitten down to the quick. We were nervous; some of our nails were bitten and chewed away. The days were long. Recess and lunch were luxuries. After recess each day, Sister had us put our heads down. We were told to rest while she took her medicine. We were obedient. We knew from experience that she was calm and relaxed after she had her medicine. She seemed to like us better after she took her medicine. With a glow about her, she emerged from the cloakroom where she kept her medicine on the bottom shelf of the thin, cream-colored tin cupboard. Her medicine always seemed to agree with her.

With a classroom full of fifty-four children, we didn't need custodians. Tasks were parceled out, one to each of us. Some days, rubber bands held steel wool on the soles of our shoes. All day, we dragged our feet, going to and from as we wished to sharpen our pencils, to throw a paper in the wastebasket, to stand in front of the room to read a report, or to go to the blackboard. This was called "Floor Polishing Day." My feet ached at the end of the day. The rubber bands that held the steel wool in place cut the circulation of blood to my toes.

Colleen cleaned the windowsills, Carolyn washed the blackboards, and David clapped the erasers. We all envied him; he got to go outside to perform his tasks. The list went on and on, it was never changed.

My weekly cleaning ritual included the thin, cream-colored tin cupboard in the cloakroom. Vases, boxes of chalk and packages of paper lined the shelves. I was to clean all the shelves in the cupboard except for the bottom shelf, where Sister kept her medicine in a dark green, thin-necked bottle. I was an obedient and observant child.

One evening my parents were having a small party. My father set up a little bar, in order that he might offer the guests a drink before they played their usual rounds of Friday Night Bridge. As Daddy lifted out one dark green, thin-necked bottle with a black VAT '69 Scotch label on it, I questioned why he was serving medicine at the party. He and my Mother looked at me in wonder.

"Medicine?" they asked in unison.

"Yes, that's the same bottle with the same words on it as Sister's medicine bottle. She takes it times every day, and it always makes her happy and nice."

My parents grinned at one another. I innocently left the room. I was confused as to why they would serve medicine at their party. It was years later that I learned the truth. VAT '69 Scotch was Sister's happy medicine.

AFTER THE STORM

THE DOG warms my feet this quiet restful evening.
Gone are the thunder and lightning of the day. Also
gone is the tidy, newly mowed lawn of yesterday. There
are fallen trees everywhere. The force of the rain has
drowned the flowers. Workmen with chain saws will
arrive in the morning to remove the disaster of the day.

The dark sky sneaked gradually over our city. We could
only watch and wonder. Hope, trust, fear, anxiety, which
were we to feel?

Tonight I sleep in my own comfortable bed with
Peaches at my feet. Others, not very far away, huddle

in gymnasiums because of floods; some stumble around their homes because they have no electricity, some don't even have flashlights.

Oxygen tanks need power for the very ill. Air conditioners aren't working where people have severe breathing problems. Families can't account for all of their members.

"Where might John be? He only went out for some milk?" I heard a sad woman say on the news.

Did the river rise to greet him? How will the people at Sunshine farm begin picking their corn next week? There's a sea of mud covering the almost developed ears of corn. The Sunshine family might have a lean winter.

Are we ever completely ready for the happenings of life? Probably not. Yet, tomorrow the sun will shine. Hope is that little four-letter word that allows us to close our eyes tonight, pet Peaches good night, and dream hopeful dreams of a better tomorrow. Hope for the happiness of others. Hope for the peace and love of God. Hope for the life of eternity where the rivers will run calmly, the thunder will be like music and the lightning will be like twinkling stars. Storms will be no more. As people of faith, we have been promised a grand tomorrow. Wipe the mud from your shoes, saw the tree limbs into small bundles and rest knowing the big tomorrow at the end of this earthly stay will be worth every bloody drop of rain, every heavy storm and all the lightning in the sky. We will be home!

"The stronger the winds the deeper the roots. The longer the winds the more beautiful the tree."

AUTHOR UNKNOWN

THE HUMMINGBIRD

HUMMINGBIRDS HAVE always fascinated me. Their tiny bodies are all a flutter. It takes patience and silence to gain their trust. Each year they return. Each spring they tell us when they are back. They arrive looking for their feeder. We rush around preparing the sugar nectar they so love. Once the feeder is filled, their behavior is fascinating to watch. They communicate with one another. They stop their fluttering and sit in our red leafed Japanese maple tree. They blend into the shapes and colors of the tree.

Early one evening, Jerry found a wee tiny hummingbird in the yard. During the day, a strong spring storm must have disrupted his tiny nest. Where were his mother, father, sisters and brothers? His wings were brilliant green. His bill was long and thin as a needle.

I held him gently. His heartbeat was fast. He was terrified. We made some very sugary water and put it in a saucer. He drank it! We laid him in the lid of a box about 12"x18". We filled the box with leaves and placed the little box safe on a shelf close to the house. We were afraid a squirrel might get him. We tried to warm him. His eyes were like tiny black dots. We put the sugar water in the box with him. We went to bed. It was late. I had hoped by morning his parents would have found and rescued him.

It was not to be. Still in my nightgown, I picked him up. He was exhausted and worn out. He had made it through the night. He took one large drink of new sugar water and then he took one last big breath. His life ended. I cried. His little life was over.

I guess God wanted him in Heaven. His beautiful colored body with his needle-like bill will flutter around in that wonderful place Christ has promised us called Heaven.

AARON

Aaron has gone from us. Off to Chicago to give
teaching a try.

I worry and wonder as I ponder the months that will go by.

Everything so new, he's all alone in a sense,
yet that all has to be.

He can stay around here with us with his dreams on
hold or go off to test his wings and his judgements.

So prepared he is and what a whiz the children of
Chicago will know not yet

What a gift they are to get!

All shiny and new so happy and sure.

He will make a difference there is not a doubt
in the life of all those about.

But why do we have to let go of someone so bright and
so loved?

Because he must go to a place to use his great talents.

He must leave the nest for now.

Life will move on at a rich pace filled with laughter
and fun.

He won't believe how Chicago will become home.

Rejoice in all he will do to cheer and
to make hear those he will take dear.

So goodbye good friend. Gone are the days of things
so simple.

The hose with which we played and ciabatta bread we spread
thickly with butter and water pistols we used on each
other each spring.

Good fun and trust were always just there.

While we played and talked and repeated galore, the stories
are clear.

We loved and we laughed and best of all, Aaron gave me
the medicine no doctor could give.

His visits filled with cheer and his ears did hear
    and he never gave up any hope.

He held my hand tightly with all his might.

Always knowing good health was in sight.

After my heart transplant, he was my light at the end of
    the tunnel

He was the rainbow at the end of a storm.

He was a gift from God.

He used the most natural of gifts — himself.

YOUR MOTHER HAS
SUCH A PRETTY VOICE

ANYTHING OVER a one night stay in a hospital is too
long. I have always been fascinated by the notion of
time. Time is so irrelevant to what is happening around
us. A rainy day can seem like a week long, while a sunny
day passes quickly. It can be over almost before it begins.

When I was in high school, I worked at the Fulton Drug
Store all day Saturday. The clock over the front door
moved so slowly that there were days I thought it was
broken. Yet, my days as a junior high art teacher flew by.

The students and I were so happy together. My 30 plus students and I were so content. I hated to see the day end.

Hospital stays for me, after all these years have become like days working in the drug store; slow, boring, non-productive. The second hand on the clock in the room seemed to drag its feet as it clicked away the seconds ever so slowly.

Last March I spent a month getting well from a staph infection. It seemed to take forever to find the right anti-biotic to fight the infection. Once the right combinations were decided upon through trial and error, the trip back to wellness took 40 days of carrying around a pump on an IV pole that delivered heavy doses of medicine to fight the disease that had attacked my pacemaker and the wire that led from it to my transplanted heart. It was a long, grueling ordeal.

I worked hard at staying on my feet. I worked hard at staying on some sort of a schedule. I worked on staying physically fit by walking the halls during those 40 days. My intravenous pole and I traveled miles up and down the halls. I knew every room and watched as people came and went.

People were friendly and kind. We were all in this together. The staff started to think of me as one of them. I knew where to find the hidden Lorna Doones and which nurse had which skills. It was a community within a community. Sometimes it worked better than at other times. Patience and tolerance were needed to face each bland, slow day.

As the days gradually slipped by, it was fun to visit with people in the open lounge areas. I had valuable, learned-from-experience information from which they and their loved ones could benefit.

Early one morning, one lovely lady sat in the waiting area. Her husband was having extensive heart surgery. Her wait seemed endless. I passed by her several times. We smiled at first and by afternoon we started to say hello. Each time I would walk by her, she was calm and content. She was crocheting an afghan of many colors. It was as colorful as a rainbow. Each time I passed her chair, the afghan was larger and larger. Finally, I got brave enough to ask about it. It really was a beauty; a work of art. We talked. In great detail, she told me that she was making it for her sixteen-year-old grand-daughter. She glowed with pride as she described in detail the beauty of her loving grandchild, Sarah. We exchanged stories. And, as the day passed, ever so slowly, we became friends. Late in the day, my husband came for his usual visit. He was full of energy and good cheer. Jerry always had news from "the outside world." We would talk and laugh and before he left, we would always take a nice long walk up and down the halls and around the nurses' station and the waiting area. I was especially excited when I saw my afghan-knitting friend still waiting patiently and working on her beautiful project. It continued to grow and grow as she looped her crochet hook round and round and in-between. I took Jerry by the hand and directed him to her. As we walked up to her, I explained to him how she planned to surprise her sixteen-year-old granddaughter with her labor of love.

We stood before her, I had on my "one size fits all" hospital gown. It touched the floor. The ties were badly worn. The breast pocket held the heart monitor. The pocket was ripped and torn. My gray hair was the best I could make it under the circumstances. I had no lipstick, no jewelry, no nothing. Sick people are stripped of the things of the world. In a way, hospitals differ little from prisons. But, having never been in the latter, I'm only making a broad assumption.

After I finished telling Jerry the story of the "fast growing" afghan, my new friend looked up into the face of my husband and with kindness and sincerity stated, "Your Mother has such a beautiful voice."

How did she know Jerry's Mother? Yes, Jerry's Mother did have a lovely voice, yet she's been dead 30 years. How had she known her? My mind raced on and on when, it all dawned on me.

My new friend had decided this young, cheerful, well-groomed gentleman in smart clothing was my son.

Years ago, Art Linkletter coined the phrase, "Children can say the darndest things." That day, as I stood before all to see in my worst of situations, I realized that grown ups can also say the darndest things! It had been a long, long day. I had done my best to get through it. I worked to keep my spirits high. Yet, as I climbed into bed, turned out the lights and waited for sleep to come, I saw the shadow of light shine into my room from the corridor of the waiting area. There the afghan continued to grow. Its maker knew not her misspoken words. My "son" got on the elevator. He headed for home. My afghan friend smiled and waved a little wave. As I said my goodnight, she said, "What a nice son you have, handsome too." I jokingly laughed as I told her he was my husband. I thanked her and said good night.

It takes a few good tomorrows to erase some of the sadness of the long, slow, sick todays.

The following day, as if adding insult to injury, a lady came to escort me to the x-ray department. Again, Jerry was visiting. Since it was late and I knew how the x-ray area operated, I encouraged him to go home. As we parted, he walked to the visitor elevator, I was wheeled the opposite direction to the patient elevators. As Jerry walked down the hall the happy attendant asked, "Now is that nice gentleman your son or son-in-law?"

Within 12 hours, it happened again. This time I decided to retaliate. "He's not my son or my son-in-law, he's my husband." I flatly replied.

"Wow!" she exclaimed.

My only reply was, "It seems as though I took better care of him than I did of myself.

She quietly pushed my wheelchair into the huge elevator. Brighter days had to be ahead.

And, they were. Today, one year later, not anyone has referred to me as Jerry's Mother. And, with a little help from things like creams, lotions, lipstick, a strand of pearls, new earrings and a good hair cut, we are both almost the same age. My "son" is my husband again. I am no longer mistaken as his Mother. Hospitals are hard on our images both physically and emotionally.

WILDA

IT WAS 1964, Wilda was 12, and she wore the same skirt and blouse to school every day. By Friday, it didn't look quite like it had looked on Monday. More and more each day, the orange skirt hiked up in the front. Each day, the orange and white horizontal stripes of the sweater stretched wider. Her bust got fuller, her stomach got rounder. She was loud and a little on the rough side. She was quick to give anyone who teased her a whack with her 18" wooden ruler.

Finally, it was obvious. Wilda had a problem. When I quietly took her off by herself, I asked if she had something she needed to share with someone.

"Well," she stated, "I think there's something wrong with me. I just keep getting fatter in strange places." She then stood up and showed me in detail why she could only wear this one outfit. She was very pregnant and didn't know what it was or how it happened. She assured me that she had not started eating anything different. Well, the time had come when she needed someone to intervene. It became my job to try to explain what I thought might have happened.

Wilda did not know about menstruation. She had never had a period. She knew nothing about her menstrual cycle. She just said, "it was 'fun' and it 'felt good.'" Eggs were something you ate for breakfast and sperm was a word she did not know.

Lovely Wilda delivered a sweet little girl in July without ever missing a day of school. When I visited her at the Children's Home, she knew her body and what had happened.

Years later I met her in a department store. Three clean, scrubbed little girls clung to her leg looking up at me. "Mrs. Whitmer was mama's teacher," she proudly told them. And, she said that since the blue paint I permitted her to use in art class was the most wonderful color in the whole world, the children were named Sky, Aqua, and just plain Blue. "When I have another child, even if it's a boy, its going to be named Turquoise," she announced.

"Remember the day you showed what would happen if we mixed blue with green? We learned to spell turquoise. That was my favorite day of school. You even had us put some white in it and it turned a lighter turquoise. It was like a miracle to me. I got to use the letter Q again. AQUA and TURQUOISE, what wonderful words."

"Thank you, Mrs. Whitmer," she waved as she and Sky, Aqua, and Blue turned to walk the mall. With hardly a penny in her pocket, she glowed with pride. She had love that overflowed in her young, healthy heart. She was never blue!

"Learning is a treasure that will follow its owner everywhere."

CHINESE PROVERB

WHAT'S AHEAD?

ISTOOD BESIDE a woman with child today. Her swollen belly was round and perfect. Never having had any children myself, I have never stopped being fascinated by the miracle of life: the conception and the gradual growth and development of a wee child in the womb of its mother.

Young mothers nestled around her giving her advice. They encourage her to take good care of herself, to use her good sense and to value every moment of the years ahead warning her how quickly the time would fly. Her child would be an adolescent and then a young adult in the blink of an eye.

Realizing the immensity of what lay ahead for her was overwhelming to me. The decisions ahead, the physical work, the emotional punches, the financial burdens, the spiritual awakenings, the days of doubt, and the fears of the unknown overwhelmed me.

The only answer to it all is in her God. He is the only constant in any of it. Of Him she can be sure. He will not disappoint her as long as she takes Him along every step of the way. Putting one foot in front of the other will move her from day to day. Building a relationship with her God will be her invested friendship that will get her out of her own way in order that the will of God will be accomplished. Become the follower, that listener that quiets the need to control, to fix, to accomplish. We must have trust in who we really are and why we really are in this temporary ever-changing world. Follow Him.

"It will fall into order. Life is like that."

AUTHOR

STEP TO THE FRONT
OF THE LINE, PLEASE

WHILE I took part in a governmental experiment as a cancer patient, I lived in Washington. Each day was filled with new experiences and adventures. There were new surroundings, new weather conditions, new people, new words, a new role. As a teacher, I directed, now as a patient, I did as I was told.

New things were obvious. Dogwood, cherry blossoms, forsythia, azalea, tulips, the size of teacups, were all blooming in March. Ohio blossoms would come much later. It was glorious. All the new things were contagious. I found myself buying brighter, lighter clothing and painting in more vivid colors.

The early months of being in D.C. were especially fun. New places encouraged me to explore new places. An herb garden outside one government building delighted my senses. I went to the zoo, the art museums and the Smithsonian.

My sister came for a visit. We went to the zoo, I had broken my leg several days earlier and I needed help. It was wonderful watching the animals in their exquisite, natural man-made environments. Because I was handicapped, I was encouraged to go to the head of the line. People looked kindly at me. It was obvious they knew something was wrong. They would step back or move further away. To the front of the line, we would go. With my bald head wrapped in a scarf and my leg in a cast, I believe they thought I had not enough time to view the pandas, Yin and Yang, in my condition if I had to wait from the back of the line.

It was a blistering, humid day. The huge air-conditioned beauty of the panda house cooled us as it entertained us. It was a delightful day, especially because we never had to go to the end of the line. People are so kind. They were quick to see my infirmities.

In illness there are some real benefits! Moving to the front of the line was great fun!

"Cast away your preconceived ideas, find a new path."

HUGRTA QUORUM COMMUNICATIONS
Glendale, California

THUNDER FILLED
THE SKY

STREAKS OF lightning flashed in the dark of night.
Like some angry animal, the evening storm roared
its mighty roar.

The peace and quiet of the beautiful summer day were
gone. The chipmunks scurried to safety in their little
homes under the patio stones, as the squirrels ran up
the tall trees to the safety of their well-constructed large
nests located in the tops of the hundred-year-old trees.
They had better hold on, the wind began to blow. It was

that kind of wind that turns the leaves of the trees inside out. The fast little creatures, so determined in what they do, knew it was time to take cover. They were ready for a roller coaster ride for sure. Can you imagine the storm from their vantage point? Wow, a real trip to Disney World's roller coaster!

Isn't it interesting how the weather storms in our world resemble the personal storms in our lives? Like the chipmunks, we need to return to safety. Like the squirrels, we need to climb to security.

Illness forces us to return home, to go back to a time and a place when things were calm and predictable. When I work with cancer patients, I often worry about those who refuse to allow their cancers to stop them in their tracks. They are unable to step away or to take shelter from the horrors of the disease. I have found that to win the battle, we must accept the ugliness that accompanies it. We must respect it. To act as though it's some little pebble in the road of life can sometimes stop the wellness process. We must honor the seriousness of what has happened. Our world has turned upside-down. We need to cope seriously with the things that will take us from the storm back to the sunny days of yesterday. Let the fight happen. Watch the lightning, listen to the thunder from within. Quiet the storm.

All else can wait until wellness is yours. You will walk out of the storm and into the sun just as sure as the chipmunks and the squirrels will rejoice in their fun-filled sunny days! Be not afraid. Face the future knowing you are strong. Free yourself. Be happy to set aside the things of this stormy day in order that the days of tomorrow will be lovelier than any before the storm began.

"A persistent longing will always persist."

AUTHOR UNKNOWN

THE WORDS WE USE

WHY DO we use the words we do? Do you dislike
the words that rushed, disorganized people use?
Words like jump, skip, run, grab are used to describe
the everyday things that need not to be done in a hurry?
Listen for one week. Listen to things like:

"I'm going to run to the store." Run? Why not walk?

"I'm going to jump into the shower." Jump? That could be
dangerous!

"I'm going to grab a sandwich." That could be pretty
messy!

"I would die for that purse." Mercy!

"I gave my right arm to have that car." Really?

Somehow, we seem to think busy, out of breath people
are important people. Important people are always
on the go. They like to think they are on the cutting
edge. Is that really what life is all about? I don't think
so. Grabbing, jumping, running and skipping sound
exhausting to me. How about you? Be careful that you
use words that mean what you really want others to hear
and think.

"I'm going to the store. Do you need anything?"

"I'm going to take a shower."

"I'm going to have a sandwich for lunch, would you like
one?"

It's all very easy — the hard part is breaking old habits!

THE TWEED COAT

I HATED THE arrival of winter. I hated it not because of the cold, or the snow or the wind or the ice. I hated it because of the return of the tweed coat.

Rough strands of wool woven loosely with specks of color between rows of colorful knots made it hang loosely and uneven. The buttonholes were frayed from years of buttoning and unbuttoning. Some of the broken rough threads had to be tucked and pulled inside the fabric with a needle or a toothpick.

As ugly and worn as it was, Mother always pointed out its one redeeming factor. It had leather buttons, and it would last us forever. It's funny how the tweed coat went from sister to sister, to aunt, and even back again. It adjusted itself to the size of whomever wore it. Sure as winter approached, the tweed coat was not far from the scene. A good shake, a day hung on a wooden hanger from a nail in the garage to air it out, and, it was ready. "Just like new," Mother always said.

Its dark brown bag color and droopy shape made me shiver with dislike. No matter, it was mine for another season. The hemline dropped and swayed. It was long in some places, short in others. The back had a seat worn into it. The tweed coat matched my sensible brown laced up oxfords. Both fought to be the ugliest.

Winter seemed to go on forever. Frequently, I would secretly wish someone might steal the tweed coat. However, it was one of those things people just don't steal. I even hoped someone might take it by accident from the cloakroom at school. No such luck. Just to be rid of it for a day would have been a little relief from under its ragged scratchy weight. Its collar rubbed my neck raw.

On wet days, the wool had a peculiar smell. The oils from the wool had a life of their own.

One day my best and loving friend, Carole, agreed to trade coats for a day. She was an only child. She never had to wear hand-me-downs.

That sixth grade day, I felt like a new person in Carole's beautiful new clean tan coat. It brought more happiness than I had ever known.

Mother was aghast when I returned from school. "Where is the tweed coat?" she inquired. It was always "the" coat, not mine, or not even "ours." After a brief scolding, I realized my day in Carole's coat was not to be forever. We traded back the next day. Yet, to this day, the memory of her new, tan, fresh, up-to-date coat remains crystal clear.

It's no wonder that now, at 68 years of age, the coat closet in our foyer brims with an assortment of coats. Like Joseph's Coat of Many Colors, I have many coats of many colors and coats of various fabrics and styles. Some long, some short, some bright, some dull. Some light and some dark. None of them are tweed!

"Loneliness is felt never seen."

AUTHOR

THE NIGHT SHE
RAN AWAY

IT WAS a cold, cold night. Darkness came early. Mother
and Mary Ann had a disagreement about something
that simmered and boiled all day. "Yes," "No," "Why?"
"Okay, who cares anyhow?" The argument brewed for
hours. Finally, Mary Ann, who was about nine years old
at the time, announced that since things were the way
they were, she would just have to run away. My mother,
determined to win this battle, replied, "Good, you just
run away. I'll even help you pack your bags."

Dresser drawers slammed, doors almost broke from their hinges. Mary Ann emerged from her room, dressed warmly in a stocking cap, scarf and her warmest winter coat. She was carrying her little brown Samsonite overnight suitcase.

"I'm leaving this place," she announced, "and won't be back."

"Good" replied my Mother, sure that she would turn back. "Have a good trip."

Turn back she did not. The front door slammed behind her. Off she went down the street. I was scared to death as I peeked out the window watching her trudge through the six inches of new snow that had fallen.

Mother talked to herself in the kitchen. "She won't go far. She'll get cold and realize how wrong she is. You just wait and see," she explained.

Time passed. Daddy came in from work. "Where's Mary Ann?" He asked.

"She ran away," replied Mother.

"She ran away on a night like this? Why didn't you stop her?"

"Oh, she won't be gone long," Mother assured Daddy.

More time passed. No sign of Mary Ann. "Oh dear, I wonder where she went?"

Mother asked. There was worry in her voice.

She called Grandma's house. "Is Mary Ann there?" She inquired.

"Heavens no," replied Grandma Casey. "She's not out on a night like this, is she?" Grandma was concerned. "Lucille, what happened?"

"Oh, she's probably at the drug store. She likes to sit up there and read all the comic books we don't allow in the house. I'll call Mr. Schaffer."

"She's not there? Are you sure?" inquired Mother. "Oh dear, Mr. Schaffer, could you look one more time, please? She's wearing a red scarf and a striped stocking cap. You know how cute she is."

"Nope, haven't seen her, sorry."

Panic took over. In any such situation, Mother would begin to sob. The sobs turned into gulps of prayer. "Oh, my dear God, help us. What have I done? I sent her away, out into the cold freezing night, alone with her precious little suitcase. I even offered to pack it for her," she agonized.

The sobbing stage moved my Father to put on his warm clothes and prepare to go out into the night to find her. Dinner sat getting cold on the stove. Life was at a standstill. Irish prayers continued to flow from my mother's lips.

"Oh, dear Lord, bring her home safely and I promise never to be a terrible mother again. Without her, I'd rather be dead. Mother of Mercy, keep my little darling safe from harm. Watch her as she trudges through the snow, keep her from harm. Don't let her freeze to death. Please, oh please, Mother Mary." She pleaded. She paced, wringing her hands, looking up to the heavens. The yellow kitchen seemed empty and lonely.

Just as everything was at a feverish pitch, Mary Ann marched up the basement steps. Her heavy boots thumped on every step.

"I told you you'd miss me!" She announced. She proudly walked through the kitchen to her bedroom. Mother and Daddy stood paralyzed! Their mouths hung open. She had fooled them-again.

She had gone out the front door, walked around the house to the back door, sneaked down the basement steps and sat in her little chair behind the furnace. She had hidden the chair earlier in the day as she prepared for her running away. In her suitcase she had her favorite book and a tiny flashlight. She had used her "run-away-time" all warm and cozy reading her favorite book. She loved listening to the scenario that unfolded in the kitchen.

As she walked to her room, she wore her usual "I won" face. Her parting words as she glanced over her shoulder were, "What's to eat? I'm starving. You can stop crying now, I'm home. I really didn't go far. It's much too cold. You don't think I'm that dumb, do you? I would have come up sooner, but I had to finish my book. It was almost as exciting as all the commotion up here! Wow, that was fun. I didn't know you loved me that much. And oh, incidentally, I can't remember for the life of me why I ran away in the first place. Oh well, let's eat, it's getting late and I have a new book to start."

Defeated, dejected, Mother shrugged her shoulders, wiped her well-meaning tears from her eyes and reheated the dinner she had so carefully planned. We ate in silence. The ordeal was over. There was always tomorrow. A new day would dawn. After all, Mary Ann was almost nine. In another twelve years, she would be 21 years old and hopefully on her own.

"Oh, Lord, make the next 12 years more peaceful," I prayed that night as I knelt beside my bed looking up to the full moon and at the newly fallen snow. "Please don't let Mary Ann run away again."

*"Know who you are and
Know where you are going."*

BILLY GRAHAM

THE GIFT OF PAIN

PAIN CLINICS are now a fairly new part of medicine. Chronic, sharp, dull, throbbing and persistent have become frequent adjectives to describe it. Doctors ask patients to describe it in every day terms. Once I told a doctor that my pain was red and rough with a variety of voices. He looked at me like I belonged in the loony bin. Another time a doctor asked how I felt and I responded, "Like Kermit the frog." Doctors often lack a sense of humor. What I meant was, I felt green and down in the mouth just like Kermit the frog always looks. Green is not a color that fits us when we are well.

I have been surprised by suffering. It fills a deep spot within us. While we try most of our lives to avoid it and run from it, it is a welcome visitor once it is fully understood. It comes quietly. Never all at once. Slowly it takes away what we thought was very meaningful. Gradually it steals what life was.

Then life becomes new. Time is slow. Quiet surrounds us. We feel inside-out, upside-down. Life is clearly different. What once happened to others is ours to realize. It is ours to endure. It is ours with which to cope. We try to pin it down. We work to address it. Along the way, we try to wrap our arms around it. We have not been taught how to do such things.

Do we give in, resigning ourselves to it as our lot in life? No, hope won't allow it. We must see ourselves as free to live in joyous rebellion against all that keeps life from becoming what God intends it to be.

Our world is filled with trapped people. People who misunderstand the goodness of illness and suffering. Suffering puts before us situations, events and experiences that draw us to release us from ourselves. We are no longer trapped people. We need the courage to allow God to pour His love into our hearts to give us the creativity, compassion, and commitment to work to have lives of good health. We need to step aside, leave the pain behind us and find a way to walk through it. Gradually, it becomes just a small part of a day. Don't let it consume a day. It will be quieted, but it takes real work. Perhaps that all sounds unheard-of. How could such things be, you wonder?

We live in a society that worships good health. Spend some time being very ill and you will see it, feel it, experience it. People, places, language everything is geared to the healthy. Shopping recently, I longed for a place to sit, not plant myself for the afternoon, just for a moment to catch my breath, to take weight from my upper body. I looked for a spot; nothing invited me to a space where I did not have to be upright. There was but a counter on which to rest my elbows. My back rejoiced for that few minutes. Shoppers looked at me in question. Shop for heaven sakes! Don't just stand there, leaning on the Estee Lauder counter. Move. Buy. Wander. Rush. Stand up straight!

Knowing real illness has given me a look at the last chapter of my life. Rejoicing in the hope that suffering brings with it. We are able to understand that suffering is an extraordinary gift. Suffering can bear good fruit in our lives. The truth of it all is that nothing can separate us from the love of God. All things will be well.

We need not fear. The future holds nothing but good, joy and happiness. We are loved. We must not allow ourselves to think that the future is full of terror or mystery. It just isn't that way. Serious illness and suffering proves that. Our glorious future is yet to come.

Hopelessness comes upon us when our future is uncertain. When we lose sight, hope frees us to live in joyous rebellion against all that keeps life from becoming what God intends it to be. Patience rewards us. Pain is a gift. Suffering has surprised me!

"All there really is, is hope."

AUTHOR

"We can do no great things, only
small things with great love."

MOTHER THERESA

THE BIRTHDAY PARTY

BILLIE HUDSON lived about a block to the west of our house on Bedford Avenue in Canton, Ohio. My sister, Mary Ann was four. She was invited to Billie's fifth birthday party. I was too young to be included. Mary Ann did not like Billie Hudson, and furthermore she did not want to go to his "dumb, stupid birthday party." Mother insisted she be a good girl and go the party. There was a hassle, as usual, about such things.

Mother scrubbed her, from her forehead to her toes, and dressed her in a pink, ruffle-shirted dress. She wore new black patent leather Mary Jane shoes with white socks edged in lace. She hated the outfit! She stomped her shoes on the hardwood floor. She marched around the kitchen pulling and yanking at the pink dress. She hated the dress, its color and its ruffled skirt. The last straw was the pink bow to match pinned in her hair.

Mother pushed her out of the front door, in the direction of the Hudson house, with a perfectly wrapped gift under her arm. Mary Ann tried to return. Mother pointed sternly for her to keep moving down the street. Reluctantly, Mary Ann arrived at the Hudson's door. Mother, exhausted from getting her ready for the party, relaxed for a moment of peace and quiet. The tyrant was gone for an hour or two. We could all get a little rest.

Just as we had started to enjoy the peace and quiet, the front screen door opened, then slammed shut. She was back! She marched into the house, determined, her bottom lip tucked over her top lip. She held her head in an "I told you so" manner.

"Mrs. Hudson didn't want me at the party. She sent me home," she said.

"She sent you home? What did you do to get sent home so soon?" Mother asked.

The phone rang. It was Mrs. Hudson. She was upset. Her voice was defensive and defeated. She said

Mary Ann had marched into the house, walked directly to the kitchen, opened a cupboard, took out a nice large soup pot, sat on the soup pot and went number one and number two, put the lid on the pot and returned it to the cupboard. Mrs. Hudson had seen the whole process and scolded her. Mary Ann's replied that was exactly where she went to the potty at home. While Mrs. Hudson was annoyed with the mess in her soup pot, she was determined to get Mary Ann to admit she was not telling the truth about always going to the bathroom in a cooking pot at home.

"Mary Ann, I know your mother and I know that she would permit no such thing!"

"Yes she does. In fact, everyone in the family does it in the pots and pans all day long."

"Lucille, I sent her home for lying to me, not for what she did. She refused to tell the truth. She insisted I did not know the half of what went on in her house and that I should mind my own business."

Mary Ann had not wanted to go to the party. She didn't like Billie Hudson, the pink dress, the pink bow, the ruffle or the black patent leather, sissy shoes! She had dreamed up a way to get out of staying at "that stupid, silly party" that she didn't want to go to in the first place.

Mother apologized to Mrs. Hudson. She fell onto the couch, exhausted, worn out. Within moments Mary Ann reappeared. Gone was the party outfit. She was dressed in her bus driver's outfit with her tin lunch bucket under her arm ready to go outside to drive her play bus up and down the street. She turned on the engine and tooted the horn. She stopped and started. She made all the sounds a bus makes as it rumbles down the street. She greeted the imaginary, make believe people and made noises of the bus doors opening and closing.

She told the people on the bus, "Move to the rear of the bus, please." She was happy in the world she had created for herself. She hated the world in which adults expected her to take part. She created her own wonderful world. It included machines, tow trucks and bulldozers. She played ball. She could run faster than any kid her age and many much older. She could pick a good fight and always win. And, she never had to go to another birthday party in a pink dress, especially one for Billie Hudson.

"Birthdays appear each year.
Be glad."

AUTHOR

MR. BROWN

AT THE junior high school to which I was assigned,
our Principal was a pal to all. He was short and a
little round. While he was never a tyrant, we knew he
meant business. We were to be at our classroom doors
at 8:00 A.M. He cleared out the teacher's lounge with
only one look. He had learned all the things that col-
leges of education taught. That was, however, not enough.
He knew kids from the inside out. He had eight of his
own. He was my hero. He was honest with me. He never
vacillated, nor did he have favorites. We knew where
he stood. His guidance was done with love. His words

stayed with me. Weeks after a conference, I would get it! He was careful to never hurt the spirit. He believed we could be better than we were. He made me believe in myself.

At the beginning of my teaching career, he told me one wonderful thing. That one thing has stayed with me forever. He asked me to believe that somewhere in those hundreds of children in that school might be a future president, an astronaut, an Olympian, or a doctor who might find the cure for cancer. I was later to discover how right he was. For from the average homely middle school of the sixties came the likes of Poetess Rita Dove, Astronaut Judy Resnick, Olympic Diver Phillip Boggs and hundreds of outstanding others. If you believe they can be great, they will be great!

"If you believe they will be great,
they will be great."

ROBERT BROWNFIELD

JURY DUTY

A POST CARD arrived in the mail. It simply stated that I was to report for jury duty. I had never seen such a notice. I had only heard people say that they had been called for jury duty. I knew nothing about the process.

Since my husband is an attorney, I was sure I would show up, be rejected and be home within an hour. It was a cold winter day. The courthouse was packed. I was given a number and told to sit in an assigned room. Out of date magazines were scattered here and there. We all sat, elbow to elbow, waiting for the unknown. Lines were formed, we were moved from space to space. Hours went by. Several times my number was changed. I went from being #123 to #63 to #3.

At each step in the process, I was sure someone would ask me about my attorney husband and send me home. I had grocery shopping to do. The day was slipping away.

Finally we were herded into a courtroom. Above the door large gold letters read "PETIT COURT/JUDGE GEORGE GREEN. An elderly lady who had attached herself to me remarked, "Oh, this is Green Court."

"No, I corrected, its petit court." I replied.

"Oh, what is petit court?" she asked.

I was aware that petite clothes were small clothes, and so I made the connection and told her,

"Oh, this court handles small things." She was sure I knew all about the court system because I had shared with her that my husband was an attorney.

"Oh, it makes sense that small offenses would be heard in petit court," she replied. We all were told to sit in the audience section of the courtroom. By this time, there were about 40 of us. Judge Green appeared and sat behind his bench. He began stating that,

"The case you have been called to hear is a murder case. At this point you need to know this in case you do not believe in the death penalty. You will be asked to judge and be part of the sentencing decision."

My new friend, whom I had told that this was to be a small offense, elbowed me and whispered,

"I don't think that's small, do you?"

Obviously, I knew "little" about the system.

"Speak softly and be sure of what you speak."

AUTHOR

MY NAME IS REBECCA

S HE WALKED up to our table where we were dining.
She had been seated at the table beside ours.

"My name is Rebecca." She proudly announced.

Her cheeks were warm and pink from a day in the sun.
Her innocent eyes were like Fourth of July sparklers.
Tightly braided hair still wet from the swimming pool
clung closely to her round, perfectly shaped head. She
would be in fourth grade in September she proudly
professed.

One lady at our table wore three strands of pearls as a choker around her pretty neck. Rebecca's eyes shown and she couldn't take them off the pearls. She reached out with one small finger and gently touched the choker.

"You look so beautiful," Rebecca admiringly told the lady in the pearls.

What innocence, what honesty! Isn't the wonder of children simply grand? Isn't it a shame that we do not carry that same joy into our adult lives? We admire things about the people we see and talk with daily, yet we usually forget to tell them of their pretty eyes, or their richly-colored hair, or their gentle voices, or their super smiles, or their lovely strands of choker pearls. Remember to admire. It doesn't cost a thing and it is ever so important.

"An act of love is so very simple."

AUTHOR

OUR WORLD

WE LEAVE the old behind in our search for being who we want to be. Changes happen. We'd like to think that we are in complete control. We are not. The work and plans, thoughts and concerns change. Big, small, trite, huge, tiny, all take on different meaning. The big concerns of yesterday instantly become small, meaningless. Why?

As the simple human beings we are, we think that like our growth patterns, or the growth of the gardens we plant, as we get taller, the more sophisticated and older we become. We know more. It just isn't like that. We are not a bed of flowers. We bloom, grow, and blossom at different times in our lives. As growth happens, we learn much. Yet, the learning can trick us. The more we learn, the more we learn what we do not know. Information and knowledge get confused with wisdom, and we seem to yearn for wisdom.

Last night a group of young people just newly graduated from various universities gathered in our kitchen. It seems that only yesterday they were innocent third graders needing me to help them use a scissors or a ruler. Like sponges, they absorbed everything I told them. Little did I realize how much they would remember!

Youth is like that. It carries with it the ability to absorb its environment, adults, and the world. Simple things get examined. Enormous things get put in place. Trust, love and joy are realized. Values that they will carry with them a lifetime emerge. They learn about integrity and honesty and they learn that there are no shortcuts. Youth devours all that surrounds it.

They witness illness and serious suffering. These demand a value system that is well shaped and firmly planted. Compassion is tested. The strength of life and all it includes is demanding. I look back today and I wonder from where the strength we need comes. For me, it has become more and more important to give to others the knowledge that they most likely will need along the journey of life. My teacher ways are just there, the need to always share and to teach. What good is it at all if we do not share it?

It is as simple as teaching a child to use a scissors. Why do we do that? Will he need it? Is need what it is all about? I don't think so. Somehow it is about caring. We care for those we know and those we don't know.

I find myself with this huge desire to do more for others. In the grocery store, I want to help an older person do his or her shopping. When, driving by a bus stop, I have this insatiable desire to pick up people, ask them if I can take them to their destinations. If it is raining, my desire is even stronger. I find myself not able to even look at them. Why am I in my nice, clean, problem-free car and they stand waiting, wet, tired, anxious to get under cover into a dry, warm place?

I have had many brushes with death. My friends' black clothing is probably worn out; it has been in and out of the closet in preparation for my funeral, many times. Each of these brushes has made me stronger. I completely believe that each had a reason. Basically it boils down to two things that are, for me, what life is really about. It is about relationships: our relationship with one another and our relationship with God. It is just that simple: how we treat one another; how others treat us; and how we love Our Maker and respect His word.

He not only told us, He showed us. He gave us to one another, friends, relatives, and children. It is all very easy once you get the hang of it. Why do we make it all so complex? It is what it is. It is not what we pretend it to be. It is not at Saks; it is not a Kate Spade purse; it is not the color of your hair, or the speed of which your new car is capable. Where do you plan to drive it 120 miles per hour?

Life is laughter, humor, silliness, an ongoing trick or a joyful memory. It is not every meant to be stormy or ugly, or full of hate, neglect, or mean spirited or competitive.

Maybe I live in an unreal world with unreal ideas. Oh, but it feels so good to be gentle and kind, thankful, honest, and oh, how wonderful it is to trust.

Illness does these wonderful things to us.

"Today our memories tell us when
and where, why and how and who."

AUTHOR

NO PERMANENT MISTAKES

WHY IS it that when we are "down in the dumps" we make ourselves more despondent by letting all the little mistakes of our life play over and over in our minds? Each thought, each tiny mistake, seems larger and larger as we let it play again and again. I worked last night at not to worry. My only consolation was prayer. God loves us. Why do we have trouble loving ourselves? Try never to be hard on yourself. There are no permanent mistakes. Even the dumbest things we do in life are not done intentionally. Forgive thyself as our God forgives us. A lovely young lady once shared with me that she has tried shaking her head real hard in order to erase a bad memory that continued to haunt her. She compared trying to remove bad memories to erasing things from our childhood "Etch-A-Sketch" toy. All we had to do was pull up the see-through cover and all was gone. Like magic, the slate was clean. It was gone forever.

"Love is as easy as you make it."

AUTHOR

OUR CANS AND
OUR CANNOTS

HAVE YOU ever thought about the things you'll never
be able to do again? It has always fascinated me
that people will be doing something or seeing someone
for the last time and they don't know it. It's thoughts
and realities like these that make me want to say a fond
good-bye or take one long wonderful look or stamp one
last impression on my mind. For, we are not, nor will we
ever be, in control of what tomorrow will bring. Because
of my new transplanted heart, I will never ride another

roller coaster or run down a clover-covered hill or jump ropes Double-Dutch style. Our "cannots" become more and more as our "cans" get greater in quality. What we can do because of the cant's are filled with the really good things of life. We can pray, love, laugh, relax, realize who our friends really are, be quiet, be creative, and be full of joy.

We have paid the ultimate price. We move through time full of courage and determination. All the time, we are pursuing our dreams. Our "cans" provide space for our wants and needs. Gone are the rushed, wasted hours of wandering aimlessly.

The "cans" will beat amusement park rides, games, and running down clover fields any day of the week. Let us rejoice in our "cans" and never shed a tear over the "cannots."

"Cast away our preconceived ideas."

HUGRTA QUOTUM COMMUNICATIONS
Glendale, California

POLLY

I ONCE HAD a blind student named Polly. She taught me some wonderful things. One cold, snowy day I drove her home from her class. Now, let me tell you, that was a trip and a half! Polly was blind from birth. She walked home to her rental apartment off campus by identifying the curbs, the cracks in the sidewalks, the mailbox on one particular corner, the sounds in the traffic. Her wonderful seeing-eye dog helped her tremendously, knowing when to stop and when to turn. In my car, I had taken away their "eyes." I used markers like "Ah, there's a yellow house on this corner," or, "There's a house with a red door and black shutters." The dog couldn't sniff the ground and Polly didn't even know yellow and red. They sat quietly.

It was indeed the grace of God that led us to their happy home. Purely an accident! Polly invited me in for a warm cup of tea. I agreed to visit a little.

She was methodical in every movement. She removed the dog's rubber boots all the while telling me why he had to wear them. The salt on the university sidewalks to keep people from slipping and sliding got between his tender toes after a long day going from class to class, building to building, thus the need for boots.

She placed the little green boots carefully in a spot that was meant for them. I volunteered to help with her books, her coat, with helping to make the tea. She permitted me to do nothing. While her place was very messy to a seeing person, she knew exactly where everything was. My urge to be "neat and tidy" would have thrown she and her blind husband into a complete tumble. He came in while I was there. His routine was much like hers. His dog's boots sat snugly next to the other pair. The dogs greeted one another with a friendly sniff. Paul fixed himself a cup of tea.

"Isn't our place pretty?" he asked. It really wasn't all that attractive, yet, I realized it didn't matter. It was what it was in their minds' view.

They had delightful stories to tell. One made them laugh as they told it. People would ask how they drive to get places. Frequently they responded. "We sit in the back-seat and leave the driving to the dogs." The picture of it all made me really laugh along with them.

Another was how people would remark, "We were going to stop in to see you last night, but your lights weren't on." So Paul and Polly tired to always remember to turn the lights on so people could see they were home!

Polly told me she had been an adopted child. Her adopted mother never made her feel helpless. Once when Polly walked through her mother's newly planted rose garden, she gave her a terrible scolding. I was horrified. After all, Polly was blind. Her mother's final words were, "You are blind, I know, but there is nothing wrong with your nose." She used strong, tough love to make Polly the strong, self-assured woman she grew to be. Paul and Polly were delightfully happy people.

On my drive home from the university that day, I was not quite the same person. I had learned the value of really living life. Over that year, Polly stretched my creativity. Designing art lessons for a seeing class that included Polly was a challenge.

Let me tell you about one very successful lesson. It was a lesson in life drawing. The seeing class members looked at the model.

They took the pose in order that they could feel what it was like to stand a certain way. We talked about the tilt of the shoulders and the slant of the pelvis, and the length of the arms and legs. Polly took part. She walked up and felt the outside shape of the posed model. The seeing class drew in pencil, charcoal or magic markers, sometimes mixing media. Polly used string, yarn and threads of various weights that I had soaked in watered-down Elmer's glue. Her hands guided the sticky string and yarns. For contrast, she worked on dark gray paper. The seeing students worked in dark ink or soft pencils on light-colored paper.

By the time the studio class was over, the entire class was working as Polly had done hers. They were excited how much more sensitive her work was. She "saw" things they had not. They loved to draw blindfolded after that. I wish I had saved the work and I wish I had taken pictures of the class. They would be perfect to include in this book. So, I guess you'll have to form your own pictures of just how unique the room looked. Some of the final works of art included Polly's dog, boots and all.

One day they did self-portraits while looking in little mirrors. I had given them sour pickles to eat. Their marvelous works of very honest real art showed the real emotion they felt as the sour pickle eased its way down through their lips, mouths, and throats. Once unblindfolded, they roared at the furrowed foreheads and turned-down mouths. One student was even unsophisticated enough to hang a long enormous tongue from the side of his mouth. They left the room all aglow. Yes indeed, fragile, blind Polly taught me much about myself and about my teaching skills. And, her classmates all loved her. In her class evaluations they wrote eloquently of the things Polly had taught them. They had no pity in their souls. They felt no sorrow. Polly would not have wanted that. The last I heard, she and Paul were working with the blind, helping them to appreciate and see the beauty in their world, beauty that many of us never really see.

"Like the person you are."

AUTHOR

PEACHES

I ONCE THOUGHT I had to make a list of the things I
did in a day. Today I realize that list doesn't have to
be filled with things I can tell others should they ask,
"What did you do today?" I no longer make those lists.
My days are filled with making memories. I spent yesterday alone. I touched the leaves in my garden. I threw
a bright yellow tennis ball to this big red creation of
God, our Irish Setter named Peaches, and marveled at
her joy in retrieving it. The small child-like brain in her
chiseled head gave her small clues of where the ball had
gone. Her thinking made MENSA look small. Her only

needs are to be happy and to give completely of herself.
I often wonder why God created this wonder just for
us! And then, after a day like this, I answer by saying,
"because He really loves us." It's as simple as that!

RED LIPSTICK

I HAVE LOVED red lipstick forever. I care not what "the look" is at the cosmetic counters. Pink, beige, maroon, or barely there. I must have clear, clean, Ingrid Bergman, Audrey Hepburn bluish red lips. Red is alive, fun; it makes me happy.

Over the years it gets harder and harder to find that special Valentine's Day red. Just when I find one I like, it becomes discontinued. The same usually happens when you find the perfect bra, underpants or blue jeans. I think it's all some sort of merchandising conspiracy.

Last winter a drive to Cleveland took us to a Saks Fifth Avenue store. My favorite lipstick was just about gone. I slowly checked out each cubical of cosmetics looking for "my" red.

A polite salesperson caught my eye and asked if she could be of any help. She had the perfect solution. She asked me to sit on her cosmetic counter stool while she went to retrieve the perfect red made "just for me." I sat patiently. It was a pretty store, a restful day. Life was good.

The nice lady returned. She removed my old lipstick, tipped the circular hinged mirror towards me and moved in close. I could feel her breath as she studied her subject. Then as she examined,

"Dear me," she said, "you must have been real pretty when you were young."

Not only did she call me old; had she called me homely? Ugly? Again, people can say the darndest things without giving it a thought. The trip home was quiet. I tucked my new tube of Valentine's Day red lipstick in my pocket. It would cheer me up. The Saks lady meant no harm. She was just being human. And, being human isn't always saying the perfect thing. Being human means we need to work to be the people we would like to be.

ROSE THERAPY

THERAPY — that time spent doing something that will correct a malfunction. With physical therapy you see actual, real results: arms work better than before therapy. Legs learn to walk. Patients thrive after very few sessions.

Music played softly as we conversed. Our leader was tall and big-boned. Her dark hair hung freely to her shoulders. Her plain face was scrubbed and clean. Her bright eyes were kind. She had just completed her work on a PH.D. in psychology. Her eager anticipation for what was ahead was obvious. She was filled with energy and excitement. Life was good.

I looked around the ping-pong table where we were all instructed on how to make a long-stemmed paper rose. I was not one bit interested. I had been a professor in a university school of art. We didn't make paper roses! I was not into Rose Therapy.

One patient was fair with a head of sandy hair that was neatly cut. His manner was easy. Somehow he seemed deep in thought. He wasn't really involved in any of the conversation. He was only half listening. His mind was some place else.

Gradually, we started to interact. We shared things about where we lived. We talked about our families, the families we left behind in our pursuits to get well. We openly discussed our cancer... where it was in our bodies, how it was detected and how we were holding up under the various treatments we were receiving.

Time seemed to pass quickly. Before we knew it, our therapy session ended. We left the room as new, wonderful friends. Each of us carried our long-stemmed rose.

After that one therapy session I had a new, wonderful understanding and attitude about "art therapy." It had brought us together. Our trained, bright, therapist found a way to get us to forget our worries, quiet our fears and communicate openly. Some listened as others talked. We became friends that afternoon around that old, worn ping-pong table.

The roses we created became symbols to us. For that one lovely afternoon, we were able to forget our troubles and learn that we are never alone.

"I was promised hope even in the worst of times."

AUTHOR

WASH AND IRONING DAY

MORNING BEGAN with changing the beds. We carried heavy baskets up and down the basement steps. Starch cooked on the stove. The blue speckled roaster held the white sticky liquid. Breakfast fit in between each task.

The day began with orders. Someone had to hang the clothesline. The hook on the tree was too high. The ladder had to be taken from the garage wall. It was heavy, rusty, and hard to carry over the step from the garage to the back yard.

The clothes props folded up and hung on hooks on the wall of the garage. If we weren't careful, a rusted metal catch that released them to their extended size pinched our fingers. They seemed to have teeth. They gave our fingers little red blood blisters.

All the wet clothes had to be hung in a special place. Whites were in the sun; dark items had to go under the wild cherry tree. The day was filled with in, out, up, down. The events of the day were ugly. If it rained, all the rules changed. Why did it have to rain on wash day?

The clothes had to come down from the lines and be taken back down to the basement. The few lines hung near the furnace were not enough to hold all the wet droopy laundry. Some of it had to be put in the unfinished attic and hung over railings. Up, down, do this, do that. Sleep came easily Monday nights.

On Tuesday, Mother spent hours ironing. She spent hours laboring over the altar cloths used in church. A job that was assigned by the convent to Sr. Mauna Firea. Sister asked Mother to keep the ironing of the altar cloths a secret from the other nuns. The fresh linens were always sneaked in the back door of the convent when no other nuns were watching.

Ironing day was long and tedious. The kitchen smelled of cooked starch and hot steam-flattened linen fabrics. Dinner was never quite right on ironing day. There was just too much to do. The kitchen table had to be pushed against the wall to make room for the ironing board; the oval willow basket, passed down from Grandma, held bundles of sprinkled altar cloths. By bedtime Tuesday night, the basket was to be empty. It felt good to forget Tuesday.

"There are songs to be sung."

AUTHOR

TAR ON MY SHOES

MARCH OF 1997. The Florida sun shone. The light of day made seeing difficult. Sunglasses were a must. The Gulf rolled up and over the white, pristine beach each morning erasing the footprints of the day before. Over and over the waves rolled in. Along the shoreline a little girl played, fascinated by the foam left after the wave returned to sea. An orange cotton hat was pulled down over her head. Dark straight hair shown around the rim. Adoring parents played with her. She ran from one to another. Her perfect body, tanned by the morning sun, moved in unison with the roar of the aqua water. Her tiny chubby feet left prints in the moist sand. Her passing happiness was contagious. People stopped to admire her spirit. She stooped to retrieve seashells; treasures she closely examined. Tiny fingers grasped them and brought them close to her face. She looked in wonder at their unique beauty. Happiness swelled. The two with her never spoke. They seemed only aware of her presence. Nothing else existed. They worshipped her.

From my chair on the beach, I watched the interaction of child and parent, parent and parent, and child to environment, the environment revealing itself with every roaring sound, with each predictable wave, as the warmth of the sun moved overhead. Within this environment, the union of these was obvious. I wondered if I were ever a child like this. Did anyone ever love me like these people loved this child? Are we able to remember this kind of love? Is it within our fiber? The scene brought back a flood of memories for me. They were jumbled and out of order. I worked to sort it out, put it in some kind of order.

One early memory was of being dropped off at Grandma's house, a quaint house on a tree-lined street. The white two-story box had a front porch painted gray. The floor had been waxed. The soles of my shoes stuck just a little bit.

Grandma had a small bed in the corner of the dining room where she rested each afternoon. Her bad heart did not allow her to go up the steps to her room on the second floor. Grandma was Irish. Deda Glenny Casey was her name and she was proud of her Irish blood. She was from a long line of Griffins from County Clair, Ireland. Her life was not easy, her mood was always filled with gloom. My hours with Grandma were long. There was little acceptance, no motivation, no creative activity planned for the day. She seemed always in pain. The hump on her back – I know today was osteoporosis. No wonder she tired easily and wasn't the life of the party.

Aunt Annie lived with Grandma. In her silent, saint-like way, she quietly cleaned the house, cooked the meals, and spent each afternoon in an old dark red velvet chair by the window reading her prayer book. Her lips moved with each word. Her head tilted. Her white hair pulled back into a full, meticulous, silver-gray bun. Her lips moved as she read her ever-repetitive prayers. Grandma slept while Annie prayed.

During the day Grandpa Casey appeared. There was never any exchange between any of them. He ate in the kitchen, alone. He sat high on a green tin stool near the sink. He came and he went. Silence. He often smiled, funny when he would return late at night. He climbed the bare wooden steps to his room holding his shoes in his hand, tiptoeing on each old step, watching to avoid the ones that made a squeak. Grandma was easily angered if her sleep was disturbed.

I was left to entertain myself. It was lonely being at Grandma's house. From an old starched pillowcase, I constructed a nun's headdress. The three-inch hem of the pillowcase covered my forehead and was pinned securely in the back. Rounded pieces of the white cloth around both sides of my face and my neck, were pinned neatly down the back. A black veil hung over it showing only the white around my face.

Aunt Mary also lived in the house. She had a dark blue wool bathrobe. On me, it reached the floor. The sash was rope-like. A stiff piece of cardboard painted white was cut to fit around my neck and hang down the front to my waist. It was called my bib. All the nuns at St. John's wore the exact outfit. I sewed Uncle Matt's black wooden rosary beads onto the cloak from my waist. For hours I played nun. No one watched. No one cared. It was lonesome being a nun at Grandma's house.

One day bored and tired, I decided to abandon the nun's outfit. It was the hot summer of 1942. I tiptoed out of the house, not to disturb Annie's prayers or Grandma's nap. Home was eight blocks away. I had walked the route with my mother. It had been clearly drawn on a map. I was not to make any changes in the walk home. I knew exactly the corners on which to stand and which direction to look. I was an obedient child.

That day, as I carefully walked the exact path home, I came to the corner at Eighteen and Myrtle. A street crew with big yellow trucks was tarring Eighteenth Street. I needed to cross. I looked down at my white double buckled sandals with slot-like decorative holes. They were newly polished with the kind of polish with the nurse on the label.

The man high on the tar truck yelled for me to run ahead and cross where there was not yet any tar. But I had been told never, under any circumstances, to leave the exact path home. And so, with all the courage of an eight-year old, I hopped from the curb, trying to take big steps. The larger the steps, the less tar in which to walk, I thought. Tar squished up over my white shoes. It filled the slot-like holes. The workmen stood in amazement. I could hear them quietly saying to one another, "Oh, no!"

Once on the other side of Eighteenth Street, I tried desperately to undo the mess. I ran the sides of the shoes in the grass in the front yard of a house on a hill. The tar didn't move. It only picked up blades of grass. My shoes were heavy with green fur sticking out from every angle.

This was my only pair of shoes. Sunday was the next day. At ten o'clock Mass I was expected to look my best. My Mother loved showing off her good little girl with dark shiny thick braids tied with red checked bows. People stopped and admired me. Would they look at my shoes? Oh Dear!

I couldn't believe how quickly the tar dried. Huge lumps of black stuck to my only shoes. My heart pounded. I spent the last four blocks in a complete state of confusion and fear. My feet were as heavy as steel. How could I disguise my terrible mistake? I had done exactly what I had been told. I had not disobeyed. I did not listen to the strange men high on the tar machine. I listened to the voice of my Mother. I wanted to be a good girl. I could not possibly show my shoes to anyone. Those shoes had to last the entire summer and summer had just begun.

Once home, I sneaked in the back door. Inky, our black cocker spaniel, was sleeping on his bed on the landing inside the back door. I carefully stepped over him as I caught the screen door as not to make a sound. Once I was in the basement, I used everything I could get my hands on to try to rid the thick black globs of tar from my shoes. Nothing worked. It had dried. The only solution was to try to re-polish them. It worked. Heavy lumpy irregular white shoes hung from my thin, little ankles. People always called me "Bird Legs." No one ever noticed the lumpy shoes. No one seemed to care. The summer seemed long. The heavy, tar-covered white shoes were awkward and uncomfortable. It would have been better to stay dressed as a nun at Grandma's. That would have prevented the tar tragedy.

I never told anyone the horrors of that day. The painful memories remained just that.

Sadness comes in all forms. Today, I can still feel the heat of the day in the tar and the smell of the tar. The image of the tiny girl on the beach returned. Were we loved the same? Indeed, we were! Today, someplace in this wonderful, wide world of ours, she has a story just like my "tar tale."

Today, I would have told someone, why didn't I then? Because then I thought being human meant being perfect and today I know better!

> *"Take joy in coming in last that others may win."*
>
> AUTHOR

JACK

WE MOVED into our home in the fall of 1981. Three or four days after arriving, there was a tiny knock on our side door. Our dog barked. I went to the door. There before me stood the most beautiful child I have ever seen. He had a head of hair so blond it looked white. His skin was like porcelain. His blue eyes looked directly up and into mine. ""May I come in and play with your dog?," this little four-year-old asked.

I asked if his mother knew where he was and he replied that she did. He entered the house. He slowly stepped from room to room, examining each as he went. He was quick to realize the house held no children, just a man and a woman and a big red dog named Meg and a cat named Sparky.

That was the day God sent a child into our lives. That child is 26 years old today. He is my friend, my confidant, my admirer, my listener, my errand runner, my cook, my car cleaner, my yard helper, and my true love. I am his friend, his listener, his very own adult, his sounding board, his confidant. We have played gin rummy by the hour, drawn, painted, learned calligraphy, laughed, gone to the swimming pool, made jam, gone to ball games, visited the dog pound and through it all, never have we exchanged an angry word.

Once, when I was very sick, it was late at night. I had been told some bad news concerning my liver. As I lay in the dark of my plain Cleveland Clinic room, I was frightened and alone.

Like some wonderful miracle, I looked up and there beside my bed was my Jack. He had called home from Boston and found out my dilemma. In his innocent youth he jumped into his car and drove eight hours to be at my bedside. It's hard to tell you the importance of his visit. He came to me when I needed him the most. We have been and will be friends forever.

God has a wonderful way of caring for people who don't have their own children. From out of the blue, he sends them to the house with a dog and no children. Kids love when they are special, and Jack was our special daily visitor. I found myself watching the clock during the day so I'd be free to play when he came in from school.

Years later I discovered he disliked his child sitter that stayed at their house until his mother returned home from her office at 5:15. Our house was his refuge. Cookies and milk awaited him. His little brother very seldom accompanied him. We always wondered why. We decided he just wasn't very fond of us.

Once Jack was off to Holy Cross College, little Aaron replaced Jack at our table for snacks and sometimes dinner. Once we were comfortable with one another, I asked him why he hadn't come to see us along with Jack all those years. Lo and behold, I learned that innocent, angelic Jack had told Aaron that we didn't like him. He wasn't welcome. He was to stay home. Jack liked being an only child at our house; and for all those years he was. We laugh today at the little fib Jack made up to protect his find. Once Jack was off to school, Aaron was permitted to replace him in our lives. God sent us a second child! Today he is our friend, our confidant, our listener, our jam maker, our cookie and milk eater, our helper, our delight!

The most exciting part of the story, I think, is that their wonderful, kind, giving parents were able to share, with us, their children. Like books in the library, we borrowed them and enjoyed them. They continue to be our enjoyment. And the best part of the story is that we get to return them when we have had enough, and we haven't had to fund their college education. They come dressed, clean, and happy. We share a love as great as if they were our own. We thank their loving parents indeed. It does "take a village" to raise children!

EPILOGUE

Wітн *Green Rubber Boots* and *For the Asking* under my belt, *Glory in a Story* began innocently enough with one very short story. I had started to miss the joy of working with words. Since childhood my mind has been flooded with the rush of stories. Experiences and events seem frozen in time.

These days since cancer in 1978, with being given only three months to live and years of dealing with a severely damaged heart from the then experimental cancer drug Adriamycin, my creative spirit seems to have soared.

Green Rubber Boots: A Joyful Journey to Wellness continues to bring hope and love to people across the country. While *For the Asking: A Joyful Journey to Peace* was written before and after my heart transplant, it seems to delight the souls desiring to be at peace with themselves and their world.

Today, as I close this, my third book, *The Glory in a Story,* I have trouble saying goodbye. It is, however, the time to say farewell to my new creation. It was written to be at your house or at the homes of your friends, not mine.

I will treasure it, as I hope you will also. It has been my friend. And so, my loyal readers, I write it for each one of you; that you may laugh and cry, think and remember, those times of long ago when you were innocent, happy, and sometimes discontented, and confused; days long ago that were filled with wonder.

Let your own magnificent memories be yours to cherish as you move on to tomorrow and all the tomorrows that will surely follow.

This ends the trilogy. Will there be more? Only God knows — I find myself hoping there will be.

However, a series of children's books sits collecting dust on my desk. Perhaps I shall move on to them. They are titled and illustrated. Be watching for them. They are:

Blue Boo

Green Gene

Maroon June

Tan Dan

Red Fred

and

Tangerine Maxine

And they are about children of color!

I might be getting too old for such an ambitious project, yet, the Lord works in delightful ways. His is to lead, mine is to follow.

"I have a song to sing for I have known miracles and miracle makers."

AUTHOR

ORDER FORM

GREEN RUBBER BOOTS $19.95
A joyful journey to wellness

FOR THE ASKING $20.95
A joyful journey to peace

THE GLORY IN A STORY $23.95
A joyful journey through memories

Shipping and Handling .... $ 3.50

Book Rate

Prints of the covers of Mrs. Whitmer's books are available upon request. Contact Peach Publications for further information.

For multiple book orders and special prices:

Call 330-867-0348

Fax 330-865-5650

Mail: Complete form with check or money order to:

 Peach Publications, Inc.
444 Burning Tree Drive
Akron, Ohio 44303

Name _____

Organization _____

Address _____

_____

City _____ State _____ Zip _____

Phone _____

Thank you for your order. Please allow two weeks for delivery.